CW01663373

The Career Confidence Toolkit

Take Control of Your Career and Fulfil Your Potential

Nicola Semple

Printed in the United Kingdom.

Some names and identifying details of clients have been changed to protect the privacy of individuals.

Written and created by Nicola Semple https://nicolasemple.com

Book design and production by Candescent Press https://candescentpress.com

Editing by Kris Emery https://krisemery.com

Proofreading by Jo Keene

Image design by Jo Richards https://greycardcreative.com

Author photograph by Vicki Knights https://vickiknights.com

For all those still trying to answer the question:

"What do you want to do when you grow up?"

For those who wonder:

"Am I living up to my full potential or just going through the motions?"

For those who lie awake at night and think:

"There's got to be more to life than this!"

I hope this book helps you find the clarity you want.

Be curious and build a career that works for you.

And if that career stops working for you,

be brave enough to make a change.

What People Are Saying About The Career Confidence Toolkit

A friend, mentor, and coach all wrapped up into one book. There's gold to be found in each chapter, and what's more, you'll get something new from it each time you read it!

Lucy Carter, *Leadership Coach and Founder of Ten Opal Square*

Simple, clear, and packing a powerful punch, this book offers so much for coaches as well as those seeking career confidence and clarity. Nicola has skilfully broken down and guides the reader through a process that (if committed to) will deliver lightbulb moments and actionable insights galore. I for one will be recommending it to clients to accompany our work together."

Jacqui Jagger, *Co-Founder Catalyst Careers*

This book is like having a career confidence coach working right alongside you. It is supportive, encouraging, and full of practical exercises. I wish I'd read this book ten years ago! It's a must for anyone asking themselves what they really want from their career and who wants to take action to get it.

Nickie Rose, *Founder of Cultiv8 Coaching and Leadership*

I loved Nicola's approach and the Career Confidence Wheel. I particularly loved the chapters on Career Beliefs and Career Behaviours. I see these challenges come up with my clients a lot(!) and I don't see enough career professionals talk about why they are so important to career success. I would highly recommend this book to anyone who wants to work on their career confidence but doesn't know where to start."

Soma Ghosh, *Founder of The Career Happiness Mentor*

This is a brilliant, straightforward, practical, and pragmatic guide to working out where you are now, where you want to get to and what the steps are that you need to take to get you there. An empowering, thoughtfully put together and thought-provoking read, this book will be useful for anyone who is feeling lost, stuck, or as though they have bounced from one job to the next, without any clear plan. Highly recommend.

Sarah Clein, *The Knackered Womens Coach*

I found it enormously helpful and confidence boosting. Highly recommend!

Anniki Sommerville, *Author of The Big Quit: How to ditch the job you hate and find work you love*

If your co-workers would say you had it all together, but you feel lost in your career, then - this book is for you! Jump on the career confidence wheel, take a spin and look in depth at the 8 key areas that will banish that lost feeling. Then watch your inner confidence grow to match your outer confidence. For me, the future of job seeking is in communities and specific industry silos and nurturing our networks, so the career village piece is gold in this book.

Zoe Macaskill, *LinkedIn Job Search Advisor, Executive Career Jump*

The Career Confidence Toolkit is a brilliant guide for anyone looking to get clarity on what they want from their career along with practical advice on how to get it. Nicola's hints, tips and friendly encouragement will help anyone looking for an easy-to-follow plan to design (and achieve) their dream career.

Elizabeth Willetts, *Founder and CEO, Investing in Women*

Table of Contents

Chapter 1

Introduction to The Career Confidence Toolkit

"Every great journey starts with a simple step."

Maya Angelou

The average person spends 90,000 hours at work over the course of a lifetime. That's a lot of time and a big chunk of our life. It's only natural that we want our work to make us happy and fulfilled. If we are going to devote so much of our time to work, we want it to give us a sense of meaning and purpose.

Sadly, this is not the reality for many people. When someone is struggling with their career direction and comes to me for guidance, one of the first questions I ask is: "Does your work make you happy?" It's a simple question that can often be difficult to answer. Perhaps the content of the job itself doesn't make my client happy, but the lifestyle it affords does. The client might love the day-to-day work but may feel like they are not being recognised and rewarded appropriately.

My clients work with me because their careers don't make them happy or fulfilled. Usually, they have never had a career plan and have got to where they are due to luck not careful planning. They are well-educated, and many have a university degree. Upon completion of their degree, they weren't sure what they 'wanted to do when they grew up'. They got a graduate job so they could get experience, did well in that job, and kept on going. If they were honest with themselves and asked if this was the career they anticipated, the resounding answer would be no!

By the time I work with them, they have got to a point where enough is enough. I've had clients tell me they've become so unhappy with their current situation that it has impacted every area of their life: their motivation, productivity, mental health, and even their relationship with friends and family. You can only 'go through the motions' so long before it starts to take a toll.

As a result of working with me, my clients decide what they need from the next phase of their career. That may be a complete change of career, navigating the transition into a new role in their current organisation, or overcoming their imposter syndrome so they can feel confident in the role they already have. Ultimately, their end goal is to take control of their career and feel happy and fulfilled by the work they do.

The Career Confidence Toolkit has been designed to help you take control of *your* career. By reading and (most importantly) completing the practical steps in this book, you can create a plan to build your Career Confidence. By taking action on your plan, you can create a life and career that brings you joy and a sense of excitement.

This book is for you if:

- You don't have a clear vision of what you want from your career. You tend to take advantage of the opportunities that come your way rather than actively defining what you want to pursue.

- You know you want something about your career to change but you are not sure what.
- You feel pulled in various directions. You have always been ambitious, and your career is important to you, but you feel conflicted because you have lots of other things on your plate as well.
- You feel a bit bruised and battered by your career experience to date. You need a confidence boost, a loving hairstroke, or ideally both.

If you have picked up this book, you want to make the most of the 90,000 hours you will spend at work over your lifetime. You desire a career that meets your needs financially and gives you a sense of purpose and fulfilment.

What You Can Expect From This Book

While I will give you practical advice, strategies, and exercises to help you build your Career Confidence, what you'll find within these pages is much more than a guide. I will give you permission to want the things that *you* want from your career. You don't need to do what your friends and colleagues are doing. You get to define your own version of success so that each day you get out of bed with a spring in your step, knowing that you are doing work and creating a life that is meaningful for you. I'll also make sure that you're not just clear about what you *want*, but also have the courage to go after it, because I want you to know you can *choose* and *achieve* your version of career success.

Throughout the book, I will use real-life case studies (with names changed to protect privacy) from my work as a Career Confidence coach. These clients are professionals just like you who have taken control and navigated themselves to a new and fulfilling phase of their careers.

The time you spend reading and completing the exercises in this book is your opportunity to pause and reflect. Your life is busy. How often do you actually allow yourself time to think? This is your chance to make a commitment to *you* and what *you want* from your future career. All the while remembering that life happens, and circumstances change. You might need to flex your plans and that is okay, because as you build your Career Confidence, you will have all the skills and resources you need to handle whatever comes your way.

What Do I Mean By Career Confidence?

Over the last few years, as I have worked with clients, I have coined the phrase Career Confidence. It is my mission to help people become career confident. But what does that mean?

The Cambridge Dictionary defines a career as:

> *"The job or series of jobs that you do during your working life."*

It defines confidence as:

> *"The quality of being certain of your abilities or of having trust in people, plans, or the future."*

Drawing on both definitions, I describe Career Confidence as:

> *"The innate trust that you can successfully navigate the world of work, whatever arises."*

I believe that Career Confidence is:

- Knowing what you want from your career and trusting that – while your career path will have twists and turns – these unexpected detours will help you learn and grow.
- Knowing that you can do your job and trusting that you can learn what is required to fill any skills gaps that you have.
- Knowing that you are doing the right work (for now) and trusting that the future will unfold as it is meant to. When the time comes you will either have or know how to access all the resources you need to make the changes you want to your career.
- Knowing you will face setbacks and trusting you have the resilience to bounce back when things don't go according to plan.
- Knowing that you have invested in building your network and trusting that your network will be there to support you when you need it.
- Knowing that your career is important and trusting that you will always do your best to prioritise the relationships that matter to you, even if you don't always find the right balance between work and home.

As you develop your Career Confidence, you will be able to handle whatever career dilemmas and work challenges come your way. In addition, your sense of control over your career will grow:

- You'll get a spring in your step and enjoy your work. Maybe it's been a while since you have felt enthusiastic about work. Once you start calling the shots, you'll feel your enthusiasm return.
- You'll stop worrying about all the 'shoulds' and 'maybes' because you know the path that you are on and nothing else matters. Having choices is liberating, but it can also be exhausting. Focusing on one defined path can provide enormous relief.
- You'll feel a greater sense of purpose and know that you are on the path to fulfilling your potential. You won't get to the end of your career and think: *'Was that it? I thought I would do so much more!'*
- You'll stop caring what other people think about you and the decisions that you make. Other people don't care about your choices as much as you think they do. Getting clear on what you want makes it significantly easier to put on your blinkers. You can make the right decision for *you*, not what other people think you should do.
- You'll identify opportunities to grow and develop, possibly in ways you had never previously considered. Once you start looking, there is opportunity everywhere and often from the most unlikely sources.
- You'll be genuinely happy for other people's career success rather than letting envy get the better of you.

- You'll get perspective about what's important and where to focus your time, energy, and attention. You'll also understand what you can stop doing so that you can free yourself up to focus on the things that matter.
- You'll be happier at home because the constant niggle of career confusion will no longer be there.

Sounds good, doesn't it? If I could, I would love to have some magical Career Confidence dust to sprinkle over people. You, lovely reader, would know, deep in your bones, that you can handle whatever comes your way in your career. In the absence of magical dust, you have this book.

How Career Confident Are You?

We are going to work together to build your Career Confidence. To do that, it's important to understand exactly where you are now. Often my clients have a general feeling of 'meh' about their career. It's my job to help them unpick and unravel exactly what is going on for them.

Some people feel very confident in their general interactions at work. However, they go with the flow and lack any sense of career direction or purpose. Others have a very clear view of what they want from their career but struggle to make it happen. Some are held back by the belief that they are not capable of achieving what they want. Others don't have the right network of people to mentor, guide, or champion them to attain their goals. To help identify the specific areas of support that clients need, I have developed the Career Confidence Wheel.

The Career Confidence Wheel covers eight key areas that – when taken together – will give you clarity on your future career direction and allow you to build the inner trust that you can successfully navigate the world of work, whatever arises.

Your Career Values - What is important to you about your work? What are your non-negotiables that you need to be happy and fulfilled at work?

Your Career Vision – What does career success look like to you? What will that look, sound, and feel like?

Your Career Goals – What specifically do you want to achieve at work in the next two to three years? How will you know when you have achieved these goals?

Your Career Beliefs – What do you believe that will either help or hinder you to be successful? What will you choose to believe to help you bring your Career Vision to life?

Your Career Behaviours – What behaviours do you currently have that will help or hinder you from being successful? What behaviours do you need to change to help you achieve your Career Vision?

Your Career Brand – What do you want to be known for? Who needs to know about the work you do and the value that you bring?

Your Career Village – What support networks do you have in place to help you achieve your Career Goals? How can you pay it forward and support others to achieve their Career Goals?

Your Career Balance – What does Career Balance look and feel like to you? What do you need to put in place to make sure you can achieve and maintain Career Balance?

I know that sounds like a lot for you to consider. The good news is that you are likely doing well in at least a couple of these areas. Maybe you're even excelling in some of them. For the rest that may require your focus, you don't need to work on them all at the same time. You can pick one, master it, and then move on to the next.

The Career Confidence Questionnaire

The following questions will help you understand what to prioritise in terms of the work you need to do to make progress on your Career Confidence. They will guide you as to where to place your time and energy and seek more support.

On a scale of 1-10, to what extent do you agree or disagree with the following statements (1 being strongly disagree and 10 being strongly agree):

Your Career Values

I know my values (what is important to me) in relation to my career e.g. flexibility, autonomy, financial security.

I know my values in relation to my life outside of work e.g. adventure, creativity, spirituality.

I am currently living my life in alignment with my values and prioritising the things that are important to me.

TOTAL __ /30

Your Career Vision

I have a clear view of what I want from my life and career.

I am not tempted to change my mind about my career when I hear other people talking about theirs.

My vision for my career is aligned with the amount of time and energy I have available to devote to it at this point in my life.

TOTAL __ /30

Your Career Goals

I have specific Career Goals and am clear about what I am working towards over the next 18 to 24 months.

I regularly track and measure my progress against my Career Goals.

I regularly review my goals to check they are still relevant and adjust them where required.

TOTAL __ /30

Your Career Beliefs

I believe that I have everything that I need to be able to bring my Career Vision to life.

I believe that I am in control of my career success.

I believe that other people's belief in me is justified.

TOTAL __ /30

Your Career Behaviours

I take responsibility for my own career success and don't wait for other people to suggest my next career step.

I set clear boundaries with others and am comfortable saying no.

I am comfortable sharing my career success with other people.

TOTAL __ /30

Your Career Brand

I can succinctly explain what I do and the unique value that I bring.

I know how I want others to think and feel when they hear my name.

I know how to share the value I bring in a way that is authentic and comfortable for me.

TOTAL __ /30

Your Career Village

I have a strong career network that I can access to support me in achieving my goals.

I have a strong support system (e.g. childcare) to give me the flexibility I require to focus on my Career Goals.

I have mentors and sponsors that provide access to opportunities that will help me achieve my goals.

TOTAL __ /30

Your Career Balance

I know what career-life balance looks and feels like to me.

I have sufficient control over my working hours so that I can achieve career-life balance.

I have sufficient control over my work location so that I can achieve career-life balance.

TOTAL __ /30

When you have your score for each category, you can plot your results on the Career Confidence Wheel.

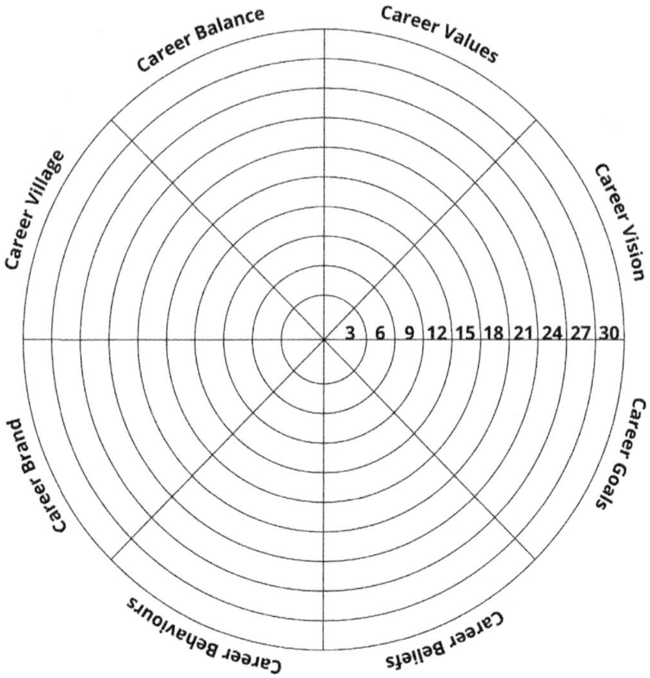

Once you have plotted your results and joined the dots, you will see what your personal Career Confidence Wheel looks like. You may find yourself with a bumpy Career Confidence Wheel, scoring high in some areas and low in others. You will easily see the areas that you need to focus on to help you improve your Career Confidence. Or you may find yourself with a relatively smooth Career Confidence Wheel. In this scenario, you can choose where you prefer to focus your time, energy, and attention.

How This Book Can Help You

To get the most from *The Career Confidence Toolkit,* I suggest skimming through the entire book first. Then, go back to each chapter and complete the reflection activities and exercises. I would recommend that you tackle each chapter in order. If there is a particular chapter that is calling to you, you could start there. However, you may come across references to exercises from previous chapters and you will need to go back and complete those before you can move on.

As I often say to clients, "I'm good, but I'm not magic". The same applies to this book. I know lots of people with extensive personal development libraries. Their reading pile teeters on the edge of their bedside table. Each night they go to bed, willing the wisdom contained within those books to transfer into their brains through osmosis. Unfortunately, it doesn't work like that.

You've made the investment of buying this book. Now you need to do something with it. The simple act of buying it and leaving it by the bed is not going to make any difference whatsoever. If you read this book from cover to cover, you might glean a few golden nuggets to help and support you on your way. As with everything else in life, you'll get the most value from this book if you do the work.

There are a number of exercises for you to complete throughout *The Career Confidence Toolkit*. I know a lot of people will think *'I'll come back to that later'* and then never do. You will only build your Career Confidence if you actually reflect and take action as a result. For that reason, I have created the Career Confidence Workbook as a companion to this book. It is a fillable PDF with all the exercises contained in *The Career Confidence Toolkit*, plus some bonus content.

You can access the workbook here:
https://nicolasemple.com/workbook.

If you don't download the workbook, I would highly recommend that you have a notebook and pen by your side as you are reading. This book is very hands-on and there aren't long stretches between 'doing' or 'thinking' prompts. You will have the opportunity to constantly apply what you are learning to your own situation.

Are you ready to build your Career Confidence? Let's get started.

Chapter 2

Being Career Confident Is Harder Now Than Ever Before

"In order to keep up with the world of 2050, you will need not merely to invent new ideas and products, but above all to reinvent yourself again and again."

Yuval Noah Harari

You might be wondering why Career Confidence is so elusive in the modern workplace. After all, people have been working to earn a living for thousands of years. The idea of a career has been around since the early 19th century when a career meant "course of one's public or professional life".[1] People have been working for thousands of years and building careers for several hundred. So, why do we find it hard in the 2020s?

The Changing Nature of Careers

Over the last two decades, the world of work has changed beyond all recognition. There was a time when you would leave school or university, start an entry-level position, and could reasonably expect to be with that same organisation all the way through until retirement. You would gain experience, take on more responsibility and progress through the ranks. As a result, you would be rewarded with a higher salary. In the world we live in, this is now the exception rather than the rule.

Our model of career progression has changed. The excellent Helen Tupper and Sara Ellis, founders of Amazing If, an award-winning career development company, have coined the phrase "squiggly careers".[2] In this new normal, people move frequently and fluidly between roles, industries, locations, and even careers. Where we start out in our career is not necessarily where we will end up. Career progression might not necessarily be linear, where we take on more responsibility and expect higher pay. It could involve a sideways move to a new functional area. We might decide to retrain. We might even take a pay cut to pursue an opportunity that we are passionate about.

This world of squiggly careers is exciting, but it also comes with its challenges. A thousand years ago, even a hundred years ago, we were born into a certain set of social and economic circumstances. For the most part, we put our heads down and played the cards we had been dealt. Only a small handful managed to break down barriers and significantly change their circumstances. In the twenty-first century, we live in more egalitarian times – certainly not perfect, but thankfully more socially mobile than at any other time in history. It is accepted that, with education, grit, and determination, most people in the western world regardless of birth circumstances can carve out a meaningful career path for themselves in any industry or profession they choose.

However, when you are told you can do anything you set your mind to, it can be difficult to identify what it is that you want to set your mind to. Unless you have a natural calling or a strong passion in a particular area, choice can be daunting.

Our Ever-Changing World

As the saying goes, the only constant in life is change. In the 1930s, economist John Maynard Keynes wrote an essay called "Economic Possibility for our Grandchildren".[3] He predicted that when his grandchildren grew up, labour-saving technologies could make a 15-hour work week possible. With modern technology to support us in the workplace and at home, Maynard Keynes suggested that one of our most pressing issues would be to decide how to occupy all our leisure time. I am sure he was a very clever man, but he definitely got that prediction wrong! I don't know many people who swim in a pool of endless leisure time, struggling to fill their day with fun and frolics!

Nearly a century later, we live in a world where we are busier than ever before. Technology has advanced in ways that Maynard Keynes would have found incomprehensible; with it, so too have expectations grown around how we use that technology and our time. Let's compare real-life scenarios from Maynard Keynes' time to now.

Buying groceries

Then: You would go to your local high street to pick up provisions for the week. The butcher would give you advice on the best cut of meat and how to cook it. The greengrocer would select your products from the shelf, ring them up at the checkout, then pack them into bags for you. Finally, you would pop to the bakery for fresh bread.

Now: You research recipes online and decide what to cook for the week. Then you go to the supermarket, load the groceries into the trolley and scan them as you go. Finally, you use the self-checkout. Before you go to bed that night, you put your ready-made bread mix into the breadmaker so you will have fresh, crusty bread the next morning.

Going on holiday

Then: Your entire organisation would close for two weeks in the summer to give everyone a chance for a break. If you were a standard Joe or Joan Bloggs, you would go to a holiday resort within an hour or two of where you lived. You would pack a suitcase, buy your train tickets, and book a B&B. Then, you would head off for two weeks of rest and relaxation with your nearest and dearest. If you were one of the gentrified few who were able to travel abroad, you would engage a travel agent to make all the plans for you. They would deliver the tickets and itinerary to your front door. Then you were all set.

Now: You book time off work. You prepare handover plans to give to colleagues who will take over your responsibilities while you are away. On your last day, you set your out-of-office message, but you know you will check your email during your holiday, just in case.

In terms of planning your holiday, with the advent of low-cost airlines, the world is your oyster. You go online to research the best destinations, use price comparison sites to make sure that you get the best deal. You book your own tickets, hotel, and car hire and you print off all the necessary documentation. Once you arrive at your destination, you don't embark on an excursion or book a table at a restaurant without checking TripAdvisor reviews.

In both examples, the balance of work has dramatically shifted to the individual. As a society we have more options available to us, which is wonderful, but it also causes mental overload. Technology and labour-saving devices have made life easier in many ways. However, the information age has pushed responsibility and work back on all of us. As a result, we are more overloaded and more stressed than ever before.

The Burnout Report, commissioned by Mental Health UK, shows that nine out of ten adults experienced high or extreme levels of stress in 2023 – a figure that cuts across almost all generations – and 20% of workers needed to take time off work due to poor mental health caused by pressure or stress.[4]

The Accelerating Pace of Change

For thousands of years, the pace of change for humans was steady and predictable. Now the pace of change is rising at an unprecedented rate. According to Michael Simmons, author and founder of the Mental Model Club, 20 years from now, the rate of change will be four times what is now. [5] For someone who is 40 in 2024, when they are 60 in 2044, the rate of paradigm change will be four times what it is now, and they will experience a year of change (by today's standards) in three months. For someone who is 10 in 2024, when they are 60 in 2074, they will experience a year of change (by today's standards) in 11 days.

A report authored by the Institute for the Future in 2019 states that 85% of the jobs that will exist in 2030 haven't been invented yet.[6] This book was published in 2024. It is mind-blowing to think that 85% of jobs that will exist in six years' time hadn't been invented five years ago. How can we possibly plan the trajectory of our career when the landscape is changing so rapidly? You may have an idea of the direction you want to take your career, but it is impossible to predict what might happen in the external environment.

Now that my children are heading into their teenage years, they are making decisions about which subjects to study. My advice to them is to pick what they enjoy. The most important thing is that they learn how to learn. There is no way to predict the job market or the specific skills that will be required when they join the workforce.

My niece was born in 1995. At the time, mobile phones were starting to become widespread in the UK. The iPhone wouldn't enter the marketplace for another 12 years. Now in her late twenties, she has developed a portfolio career encompassing her various interests, one of which is user interface design. She uses her expertise to enhance the customer's experience of websites and apps. Who could have predicted *that* in 1995? We had never heard of an app!

Another niece was born in 2000, four years before the launch of Facebook. Now in her early twenties, she has a highly successful career as a social media influencer. She has almost 400,000 followers on TikTok and a plethora of sponsorship contracts and collaboration opportunities. Her current career direction would have been impossible to predict when she was born.

The Growing Challenge of Confidence

As the career landscape becomes more complex, our level of confidence to navigate that landscape is diminishing. Independent body My Confidence

Matters conducted research with the University of Glasgow[7] and found that 79% of women and 62% of men often lack confidence at work. Of all respondents, 61% said they *appear* confident but don't *feel* confident. This is an important distinction. We can learn how to adopt behaviours that allow us to *appear* confident. However, we might lack the inner confidence and self-belief required to *feel* truly confident. There are a number of factors that contribute to this lack of confidence epidemic.

Analysis paralysis

The changing landscape provides access to a range of exciting opportunities. However, increased choice makes decision-making more complex and can lead to analysis paralysis. Analysis paralysis is the continuous overthinking and overanalysing of each career option. You spend all your time thinking about what you want from your career and waiting for the perfect opportunity to come along, rather than taking action and doing something about it. This means that months, even years, can pass and no progress is made.

This can look like: I'm so fed up with my job. I need a change. In fact, I'm not just fed up with my company. I'm fed up with working in finance. But if I were to do something different, what would it be? I've always been interested in HR, maybe I should retrain? Can I afford to take time out to study? What if I do take time out to retrain and I don't enjoy that either? What a waste of time! Will I even be able to get a job if I don't have relevant experience? Even if I get a job, I will have to start over. Will I get paid enough? Maybe HR isn't the right path. Maybe I should consider financial consulting?

Fast forward one year and you find yourself in exactly the same place with no plan of how to move forward.

Other people's opinions

No matter what you decide to do with your life, somebody will not agree with your choices. It could be a parent, partner, sibling, child, friend, or colleague. At some point, someone will think you're making a poor choice, and you should do something else. Keep in mind the rate at which the world is changing. Those around you might not understand the opportunities available to you. Friends and family want to keep you safe and so discourage what they don't understand.

It can be hard to have the confidence to do what you want to do when a seed of doubt has been planted. Who are you to pursue a promotion? Who are you to juggle work while studying for a qualification? Who are you to have a young family and continue to work full time? Thought leader Marianne Williamson wrote:

> *"We ask ourselves, who am I to be brilliant, gorgeous, talented, fabulous? Actually, who are you not to be?"*

This is a beautiful and empowering thought. Yet when loved ones hint or tell us that we aren't brilliant, gorgeous, talented, or fabulous, it can be hard to maintain the belief that we are. And so, even if we begin to get closer to understanding what we want from our life and career, we might find ourselves pulling back from it. If other people don't think that we are capable of such things, then perhaps they are right and we shouldn't even try. Blocking out the opinions of other people is a tall order. It requires confidence, gumption, and a dash of bloody-mindedness.

Our tendency to compare ourselves to others

Human beings are naturally curious. We are interested in – and dare I say a little nosey about – what is happening in the lives of those around us. In the past, we used to camouflage ourselves behind net curtains. We would look out into the street, checking what the neighbours were up to and hoping we wouldn't get caught. Now, social media has given us an all-access pass into each other's daily lives. This is having an enormous impact on our ability to figure out what *we* really want from *our* own life.

We fear looking silly, making mistakes, and having the whole thing recorded, broadcast, and shared across the internet. As a result, we are less willing to take risks, try things out and be who we really want to be. How will you know if you want to be an inspirational speaker if you don't give it a try? Once upon a time, the concern was that you would make a fool of yourself in front of everybody in the room. Now your humiliation could be shared with everybody in the room and the rest of the world as well!

We can spend so much time looking at other people's lives and experiences rather than focusing on the things that we want from life. This can lead to:

- **Feeling inadequate**. You look at all the amazingly interesting things your friends are doing. You are not doing anything like that. Your life is 'boring' in comparison (when actually the 'boring' life you have might be exactly what you want).

- **Feeling that everybody else is doing it, so you should too.** If everyone around you is getting married, having a baby, getting a promotion, or moving house, you might feel like you should do the same. If you don't have a clear vision of what you want from life, it can be very difficult or even impossible to avoid getting caught up in a wave of 'keeping up with the Joneses'.

- **Feeling that nobody else is doing it, so you shouldn't either.** If you can't see anyone else doing the thing you want to do, perhaps it's a silly idea. Even if it's a great idea, you might not want to stand out from the crowd and be considered different.

- **Feeling overwhelmed and confused.** Coming back to the earlier point about the amount of choice available to us. Our social media feed could be a source of endless inspiration. *Look at all the amazing things that my friends and contacts are doing!* Or it can be a source of confusion and overwhelm. *Look at all the amazing things my friends and contacts are doing. Ahhhhhhhh! I'm not doing any of these things. Should I be doing these things? Which of these things should I be doing? How would I ever find the time to do any of these things?* You might jump from one thing to another without following through on anything. You are endlessly 'inspired' by what others are doing rather than focusing on what you want to do.

With all of that in mind, is it any wonder that building your career with confidence in this ever-changing world is bloody hard work? Having a career means something completely different today than it did even 10 years ago. We can't just tell ourselves to "be confident". The environment and circumstances conspire against us to feel anything but.

The world is changing at breakneck speed, making it hard to plan ahead, even by a few years. The key to the future is learning and reinvention. We will constantly need to relearn and expand our skillset.

We need to be open to gaining knowledge and learning new approaches and ways of working. We should keep our eyes and ears open and seek out opportunities to continue our development. Lifelong learning is no longer a nice phrase to stick on your CV to make you sound progressive. It is a fundamental career necessity. Developing self-awareness and equipping yourself with tools and strategies are crucial for career success. You will need these skills to navigate the relentless pace of change.

In a Nutshell

- The world of work is changing more quickly now than ever before. We know that the vast majority of jobs that will exist in 2030 did not exist in 2019.
- The information age has shifted work to individuals. This has left people feeling overloaded and stressed.
- The pace of change is rising rapidly. In 2044, the rate of change will be four times what it is now.
- People are losing confidence. They doubt their ability to navigate this complex career world. The lack of confidence in the workplace is more pronounced in women, with almost four in five lacking confidence, compared to three in five men.
- This lack of confidence epidemic is a result of: increased choice, making decision-making more complex, leading to analysis paralysis; influence from the opinions and expectations of others; comparison to other people and adopting other people's model of career success.
- It's now impossible to make long-term career plans. Learning and reinvention will be key. Self-awareness is therefore crucial. As is building a collection of tools and strategies for career success.

Chapter 3

Your Career Values

"When your values are clear to you, making decisions becomes easier."

Roy E. Disney

Do you remember the sticks of rock you used to buy in seaside gift shops? When you broke them open, there would be a word, or words printed through the length of the rock. Your values are like these words. They are the fundamental beliefs that motivate and guide you. They determine what is important and run through every single thing you do. They are deep-rooted and held in the core of your being.

Your values are what is important to you. They define the type of person you want to be. They influence how you interact with the world around you and how you treat people. Some of your values will form in early childhood and stay with you for your lifetime. Others will change and evolve. Essentially your values are what makes you the person you are.

When we talk about values, we talk about them within a specific context of our life, such as career, family, health, spirituality, and so on.

What we value in one aspect of our life might not be what we value in other aspects of our life.

In the context of family, 'routine' is one of my values. I know that my family thrives when we have a set pattern to our days and weeks, and everybody knows what is happening and when. However, in the context of my career, I value 'variety'. In a work context, I find routine restrictive and dull. My ideal scenario is for no two days to be the same. I have built my business around a diverse portfolio of roles so that I can minimise routine. I can tolerate a little more routine at home, knowing I have variety when I am at work.

Your Career Values represent your beliefs about what is important to you in the context of your work. Understanding your Career Values can bring a huge sense of relief. Once you have clarity on what is important to you and what you stand for, your Career Confidence grows. Without knowing your Career Values, it can be difficult to know what decisions to make and which direction to take.

When we are connected to our Career Values, we can tap into a source of internal motivation. We may appear to achieve success – for example, finishing a project, getting promoted, or being paid well. However, it *feels* fulfilling and satisfying when it aligns with our values. Think about the hundreds of thousands of healthcare workers on a low wage. They have not chosen to join that profession because of the salary. They have chosen that career path because it aligns with their values of caring for and helping others.

The Importance of Knowing Your Career Values

Knowing your values helps you to:

- Understand yourself
- Understand the world around you
- Make decisions easily and effortlessly
- Stay motivated to pursue your goals

Understanding Yourself

Knowing your values helps you understand why you may behave and respond to situations in a particular way. For example, if you value 'adventure', you may be happy to move organisations and change roles every two years. If you value 'stability', you may be happier staying with one organisation in the same role for long periods. Both scenarios are perfectly valid. Knowing your own values will help you understand why you do the things you do.

Understanding the World

Once you start to understand your values, it helps you to understand the world around you. You perceive the world through your own specific lens, which is created based on your experiences, beliefs, and values. You can also start to consider why other people behave differently to you. I have a client whose highest value is security, both in terms of job security and financial security. When she is making decisions about her career, this is front of mind. She is willing and happy to forego the opportunity to work abroad or to diversify her skillset. Her highest priority when making a career decision is maintaining her sense of security.

Making Decisions Easily and Effortlessly

Knowing your values is your shortcut to making the right decisions for you. When presented with a range of options, it can be tricky to know which one to pick. When you know your values, you can assess each option based on whether it aligns with your values. Then, you can quickly eliminate things that will not make you happy. Consider your values to be your North Star or your guiding principles. Making decisions becomes much easier when you're clear on what is important to you.

Staying Motivated to Pursue Your Goals

Staying on track and working towards specific goals can be challenging. Being clear on your values helps to provide momentum to keep you focused and take action. When your values align with your goals, you know why you want to achieve these things. When my children were very young, my number one career value was 'flexibility'. Above all else, I wanted to have the flexibility to be able to put my family first, no matter what. For me, this meant building up my own portfolio career on a self-employed basis. It wasn't easy! At times, I wanted to give up. I wanted a safe, steady salary deposited into my bank account each month. However, I had to keep refocusing on my value of flexibility and my desire to maintain control over my own time and work location.

Values in Action

My client Abigail's highest career value was 'location independence'. She enjoyed the freedom of being able to spend the majority of the week working from home as this allowed her to spend more time with her two young children. A couple of months into our coaching relationship, her CEO wanted her to apply for their head of international sales role. It would be a promotion and a higher salary. My client was incredibly flattered. However, she was based in the UK and the new role would mean that she would need to spend a week a month in Houston, Texas.

We had already worked on her values. We were able to go back and test this role against her values and what she believed to be important to her. She felt excited about the pay, promotion, and international travel. However, having significant periods away from her family on an ongoing basis was a sacrifice she was not willing to make. Rather than get swept away in the excitement, she used her self-awareness and values to make a decision that was right for her and her family.

She told her CEO that if the opportunity came up in five years, she'd jump at it; right now, though, it wasn't right for her. Her CEO respected her decision. Over the next year, they adjusted her role to challenge and stretch her without the burden of international travel and time away from home.

Where Do Our Values Come From?

Our values develop in childhood and throughout our teens. By the time we enter the working world, we already have a fully developed set of values. It's important to note that our values evolve over time based on our experiences and circumstances. We can also consciously decide to reprioritise our values. For many of my clients, purpose and a sense of fulfilment comes high up their list of Career Values. However, the post-Covid cost of living crisis has caused them to re-evaluate their priorities; while purpose and fulfilment are still important, financial security has taken priority, at least in the short term.

When Susie was identifying her values, she initially put 'contribution' at the top of her list. Supporting others and making a positive contribution to the world were incredibly important to her. In our first coaching conversation, we had talked about how she wanted to move to a bigger house so that her children could have their own bedrooms. I queried why generating wealth or at least financial security wasn't on her list of Career Values. Without money, she wasn't going to be able to buy that bigger house. She shared that when she was growing up, she was led to believe that wanting to be wealthy made you greedy. She was also taught to be grateful for what she had, rather than aspire to have more. If she was being honest with herself, generating wealth *was* important to her. She wanted to be able to give her family the life she desired for them, but she had an ingrained belief from her childhood that she shouldn't value money.

There are no right or wrong values; only what is true for you. It is important to be completely honest with yourself, otherwise your career will not give you what you want. Your values will be an important foundation for your Career Goals. They will also be a key reference point for the career decisions you make. Therefore, you need to be deeply honest with yourself about the values that are truly important to you.

How Do You Identify Your Career Values?

Many people find the concept of Career Values vague. This might be the first time you have ever thought about your values, and you may find them difficult to define. You might need to do a little bit of detective work to uncover what is important to you.

Create your Career Timeline

As a first step to uncovering your values, review your career history. Reflecting on it can provide interesting insights into what is important to you about work and career. To create your Career Timeline, map out your career from your very first job to the present day, even if it's unrelated to your current work. Then identify the highs and lows of your career and take time to reflect on what caused those highs and lows. Have some fun and use it as an opportunity for a trip down memory lane.

When I look at my own personal Career Timeline, one of the career highs for me was my very first job when I was 15 working as Saturday assistant in a pharmacy. I was quickly given a lot of responsibility and found myself joining the regional team calls and reporting the weekly sales figures. I loved that the pharmacy manager had taken a risk on me. I felt a sense of responsibility knowing other people were counting on me.

One of my career lows was in the early days of my consulting career. I was assigned to a project configuring an Oracle database. I couldn't see how the work I was doing fitted into the overall project. I was coming into the office each day, not enjoying the work, and feeling no sense of purpose.

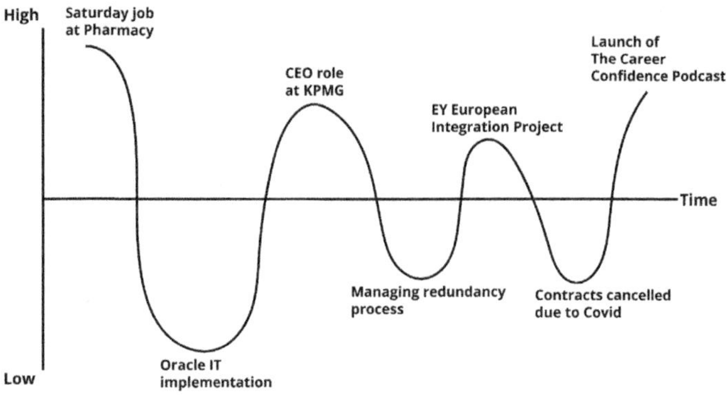

From reflecting on both situations, I can see that 'making a difference' and 'making a contribution' are two values that are important to me. Build up that picture for yourself and take some time to notice any of the key themes that come up for you.

Identify what is important to you

The next step is to identify what is important to you in relation to your career. You might break down those important things into categories such as:

- People I work with
- Place of work
- Content of role
- Type of organisation
- How work fits into my life

Career values are things like:

Achievement	Freedom	Motivation
Ambition	Friendship	Openness
Challenge	Growth	Potential
Communication	Happiness	Power
Contentment	Harmony	Professionalism
Creativity	Humour	Quality
Empathy	Independence	Stability
Enjoyment	Integrity	Trust
Fun	Kindness	Teamwork
Flexibility	Loyalty	Transparency

Brainstorm the things that are important to you using your own words.

There are no right and wrong answers here. There's no need to use formal language. The important part of this exercise is that you know what it means and why it is important to you when you look at the word.

Keep reviewing and refining this list, you might start to notice patterns or recurring themes that you can group under a single heading. You aim is to have a list of 8-10 key Career Values.

Prioritising Your Values

The next step is to prioritise the values you have identified. Look at your list of values and ask yourself: "If I could only have one of these things, what would it be?" In an ideal world, we would want our career to fulfil all these values, but keep in mind that we do need to prioritise at this stage.

Once you identify the first value on your list, look at the remaining ones and ask yourself: "If I could only have one of *these* things, what would it be?" Do this until you have a complete list of prioritised values.

When I do this exercise with clients, often the values they think are going to be their top priorities end up not being so important to them. Sometimes, those values can be removed from the list altogether!

Further Prioritising Your Values

You now have a prioritised list of 8-10 values. Well done! This isn't easy and you are doing brilliantly to have got this far.

Now we are going to get even more ruthless to validate the priority order of your values.

Take Value #1 on your list and ask yourself: "If I had Value #1, would it be okay not to have Value #2?" For example, if I had flexibility, would it be okay to not have recognition?

It's important to understand that no one is saying you can't have Value #2. We are just trying to identify if Value #1 or Value #2 is more important to you. In this case, would it be more important to have flexibility than recognition?

Move through the list and ask yourself this same question for all your values. Reorder and reprioritise your values as you go. In doing so, you'll get a better sense of your priorities. In the end, you should be able to identify 3-5 values that are most important to you.

From there, you can start to explore what that value means to you and why it is a priority. Use this as a journaling prompt. Ask yourself: "Why is X important to me?" Without overthinking, start to write and allow thoughts to arise without filtering them.

It might take you a while to come up with your key values. You may need some time to ponder and reflect to identify the right list for you. You might need to revisit this exercise over time to reflect on whether anything has changed for you.

Knowing your values is the foundation of building your Career Confidence. Understanding what is important (and what is not) helps you gain clarity around what you want from your career. It also helps you build trust in yourself and your ability to make decisions.

In a Nutshell

- Your Career Values represent your beliefs about what is important to you about work.
- Understanding your values helps you to:
  - Understand yourself
  - Understand the world around you
  - Make decisions easily and effortlessly
  - Acknowledge your successes
  - Stay motivated to pursue your goals
- To identify your Career Values, you will first create a timeline of your career, mapping out your highs and lows, then note what is important to you, looking at the people you work with, the place you work, the role, the organisation, and how work fits into your life.
- When you prioritise your values, you will narrow down the key values to a maximum of 10, then go through a two-stage process of refining the order.

Chapter 4

Your Career Vision

"Your vision will become clear only when you can look into your own heart. Who looks outside dreams; who looks inside awakes"
Carl Jung

Do you know what you want from your career? Or as that famous 90s girl band would say, what you really, really want? As we embark on the journey of building your Career Confidence, it is super important that you take the time to reflect on what *you* want. Not what you think you should want or what other people want for you. You need to create *your* Career Vision. By vision, I mean a way of articulating what you want from your future career.

Specifically:

- What will you spend your time doing?
- Who will you spend your time with?
- What will that version of your career feel like?
- What will your career allow you to do or enable you to have?

I know they feel like big questions, and they are, but they are important questions.

Many people fall into their career. They don't know what they want to do when they grow up. At the start of their career, they take a job that sounds reasonably interesting and matches their relatively limited skillset. They proceed to do well in that career, perhaps getting a promotion or two. While the work doesn't particularly excite them, they keep on keeping on. If they weren't doing this, they have no idea what they would do instead. If this sounds familiar, please don't be disheartened. You are not alone.

I want you to imagine two scenarios to help you understand the power of creating a vision for your career.

In the first scenario, you have a day off work. You're not sure what you want to do with the day, so you decide to go for a drive. You don't know where you are going, but the weather is beautiful, and you are keen to hit the open road. You head towards the coast; you pull into the first car park you come across, you see a slightly dishevelled ice cream van and decide you will chance it. You walk down the pathway to the beach only to discover the tide has come in, so you spend a short while admiring the view from the top of a sand dune, while finishing your ice cream.

A few more minutes pass. You start to worry you will get stranded on the sand dune, so you decide to return to your car and drive along the coastal road. You happen upon another ice cream shop with a sign celebrating their award for Best Ice Cream Shop in the UK. You notice crowds of people enjoying their ice cream. Others are climbing up to a lookout point on the hill, where you imagine the view out to sea would be outstanding. You consider stopping, but you've already had an ice cream and now you want to go home. When you arrive home, you think to yourself that given you had no expectations, you've had a rather nice day.

In the second scenario, you have a day off work. You know you want to make the most of the beautiful weather. You've been working from home for the last week, so you are keen to go for a drive and get some fresh air. You want to come back feeling relaxed, refreshed, and like you've had a mini adventure. You're a sucker for ice cream. You Google "best ice cream south coast" and find the details of the Best Ice Cream Shop in the UK. You key the location details into your satnav and head off.

When you arrive at the ice cream shop, you decide to take a walk up to the lookout point where the views are out of this world. When you survey the beautiful seascape spread out at your feet, you get a feeling of deep peace. You inhale the restorative sea air. You enjoy a delicious ice cream. It's one of the best you've ever had. You make a mental note to tell your best friend about the place. You know that she will love it too. You get back into your car feeling happy and replenished. You arrive home feeling peaceful, relaxed, and satisfied that you have made the most of your day off.

In both scenarios, you have had a nice day. However, in the first scenario, you missed opportunities to check out the view from the lookout point. You also missed the chance to sample the best ice cream in the country. In the second scenario, you knew what you wanted to get from the day. You did some research and put some thought into making sure you got it.

If you fall into your career and take opportunities as they arise without much forward-thinking and planning, you may still enjoy success and satisfaction. However, if you know what you want from your career, you can take focused action to create a career that fulfils you.

What Do You Want From Your Career?

When I ask clients what they want from their career, I am often met with a blank stare. If I had a pound for every time I got the response *"I just don't know"*, I would be a very rich woman. Well, perhaps not very rich, but I would certainly have enough to treat myself to a luxury Italian getaway with an unlimited supply of gelato.

It seems crazy that so many people don't know what they want, but it makes perfect sense. The clients I work with are professionals. They are highly educated and by objective standards lead a privileged life. With this privilege comes the ability to make choices, which is again a great position to be in. However, it can also be incredibly difficult to decide which choice to make.

Here is a simple example. You go into a shop to buy ice cream. The choice is between vanilla and chocolate. It's an easy decision. However, if you were to go into a shop and the options are vanilla, chocolate, salted caramel, mint choc chip, honey and ginger, bubblegum, raspberry ripple, and cookies 'n' cream, I am going to wager it will be harder to make a decision. Although, I think we can all agree to rule out bubblegum flavour pretty quickly!

My clients have multiple career paths they can pursue. They can:

- Stay with their current organisation but move to a different department
- Pursue a similar career in a different organisation
- Use their existing skillset and move into a different industry
- Work for a startup
- Start their own business
- Return to education and retrain

The list goes on!

It is wonderful to have so many options available. However, trying to choose the right one can be stressful. Making choices requires us to trust ourselves and be comfortable that we know what is best. This can be a challenge for many people. In the worst-case scenario, it can lead to analysis paralysis, as outlined in Chapter 2, which results in not making any changes and staying stuck.

Over the course of the next few chapters, I want to help you reflect on what is important for you and work out exactly what you want from your career. Before we do any of that, I'd like you to take time to consider where work fits into your life and what is feasible for you in terms of your career right now.

Seasons of Your Career

Your ambition might be urging you to focus on your career, but there might be other things going on in your life that mean it is not be the appropriate time for you to push ahead. We can learn a lot from nature. Spring is the season of growth. Summer is the time to enjoy the fruits of our labour. Autumn is the time to reflect and retreat. Winter is the time for hibernation and rest.

Much as we experience seasons of the year, we also experience seasons within our careers. There will be times when we have fewer commitments elsewhere. During these times, we can focus our time, energy, and attention on our career aspirations. There will be times when we have other areas that take priority, like caring for small children or elderly relatives, or dealing with physical or mental health issues. In those times, we have to divert our time, energy, and attention away from work to other aspects of life. Your career is a marathon, not a sprint. It's okay for you to move at a slower pace when circumstances demand. And equally, there will be times when you have more space in your life to pick up the pace and accelerate your career progress.

A few questions to ponder are:

- What season of your life are you currently in?
- To what extent are you able to devote time, energy, and attention to your career as you would ideally like?
- How might the season of your life influence your Career Vision over the next 3-5 years?

What Does Career Success Mean To You?

The author Anna Quindlen hit the nail on the head when she said: "If your success is not on your own terms, if it looks good to the world but does not feel good in your heart, it is not success at all."

What does success look like to you so that it feels good in your heart? If you want true career success, it is important to get clear on the purpose and direction you want to go with your work. Also, consider how your work fits into the wider aspects of your life.

Life is busy. We can get swept up in our day-to-day routine and find ourselves working towards unimportant goals. If everyone around us is working long hours and focused on that next promotion, aiming to afford a bigger mortgage, pay for school fees, or fund foreign holidays, it's easy to get swept along and think we should do the same.

For a lot of people, knowing what they want isn't clear cut. Often people find it easier to define what they don't want rather than what they do want. This provides a helpful starting point. However, you need to define what you *do* want, so you know what you are working towards.

Consider the following questions:

- **What does career success look like to you?** Be honest with yourself. You're not looking for the answer you think you *should* have or the answer that is the norm for your friends and colleagues. You want to find your unfiltered, unedited response.
- **What do you want from your career over the next 3-5 years?** Don't try to look any further ahead than this. As we identified earlier in the book, the world of work is changing rapidly. Your personal situation and family dynamics will constantly change. Keep in mind your current season of life and how that might impact your career plans over this period.

To get into the detail around what that career success looks like you can:

- Map out your ideal day or week
- Understand your financial motivations
- Know your strengths
- Consider your aspirations for development

Mapping Out Your Ideal Day or Week

Create your vision of your ideal day or week. For some people, a day makes sense as there is an element of routine to the work they do. For others, the type or location of work they do may vary throughout the week, so it's helpful to look at the week as a whole.

This is an opportunity to use your imagination and get creative about how you want to spend your time. You can also be highly practical, getting into the nitty-gritty and logistics of your day.

- What will you spend your time doing?
- What time will your day start?
- How many hours will you work each day?
- Where will you carry out your work?
- If you don't work from home, how long is your commute?
- Will you work alone or as part of a team?
- Will you manage other team members?

- Will you have a lot of responsibility?
- Will your work involve travel?
- How will your work fit with other family commitments?

Understanding Your Financial Motivations

Building a successful career is not just about the amount of money that you earn. However, you need to put food on the table and a roof over your head. Money needs to be part of your consideration of what career success looks like to you. Give some thought to these questions:

- How much do you need to earn?
- How much do you want to earn?
- What is the gap between what you need to earn and what you want to earn?

You are creating your vision of career success. You get to pick what financial success looks like for you.

Another interesting insight is to ask yourself what sacrifices you are willing to make to achieve what you want to earn versus what you need to earn. Are there elements of your ideal working day that take a higher priority than earning what you want to earn as opposed to what you need to earn? This helps to unearth your priorities. It shows what you are willing to give up in order to earn more money.

For example, would you accept a lower salary than you would ideally want so that you could permanently work from home? Or so that you could work a four-day week? Or so that you could walk to work each day? By answering these questions, you are adding more detail to the picture of what career success means to you.

Sarah was very successful in her Account Manager role. She was on track for a promotion to Senior Account Manager, but she wasn't sure it was what she wanted. We worked together to help her come up with her medium to long-term Career Vision.

Sarah felt that her current role didn't allow her to express herself creatively. As a student, she had always pursued creative endeavours. She felt this was lacking in her everyday life. She wanted to explore the possibility of pursuing a more creative career path. Sarah was able to define her values and started creating her longer term Career Vision. However, answering the questions "how much do you need to earn?" and "how much do you want to earn?" helped Sarah get clarity about what she really wanted from her future career.

Sarah knew how much she needed to earn to cover her rent and sustain her current lifestyle. However, she was keen to buy her own flat and build up a nest egg to allow her to take a sabbatical and travel. If she followed an alternative career path, Sarah knew she wouldn't be able to enjoy the same financial security. A promotion in her current organisation would allow her to have that. She decided that financial security was so important that she was willing to sacrifice a creative aspect of her day job. She then committed to a weekly art class and a week-long painting retreat. This helped satisfy her need for creativity, while her day job provided the income she needed to support her desired lifestyle.

Knowing Your Strengths

A successful career is one where you can play to your strengths and are supported in the areas that don't come so easily to you. Most people can name at least one or two things they are good at. This is an opportunity for you to delve deep and understand all your strengths.

Data gathering

Go back to the Career Timeline you created in Chapter 3. This time, review your Career Timeline through the perspective of the skills and strengths that you brought to each situation.

- Identify times when you performed well compared to other people with similar experience to you. Don't compare yourself to somebody who has 10 years more experience than you do, as that's not a fair comparison.
- Identify the 'bright spots', the times when you produced excellent results. Which of your strengths did you use to help you produce those results?
- What do you do that doesn't feel like work to you?

We often don't notice our strengths because it feels easy and natural when we are good at something. However, what feels easy and natural to us does not feel easy and natural to everyone.

It's also important to get an outside perspective. A good source of data is your performance review and any other on-the-job feedback. What key themes emerge? Ask other people for feedback. This doesn't necessarily have to just be people from work. You want to develop a rounded view of your strengths. Consider who has seen you operate at your very best. This could be colleagues, managers, mentors, social club members, family, friends, etc.

It can feel uncomfortable to ask for this kind of feedback. However, people love to share their opinions and you may be pleasantly surprised by the outcome. You may even inspire the people you ask to carry out their own strengths exercise. To make sure you get consistent feedback from the people you ask, I would suggest sending a very simple message:

Hi X

I'm doing some work to figure out what I want from my career and I'm asking people I know to tell me about when they've seen me at my best. I'd love to have your input.

Could you please take a few moments to share with me a time (or times) when you have seen me at my best.

I'd really appreciate it!

Aim to send your request to 15-20 people. That may seem like a lot, but keep in mind that not everybody will reply or reply within the timeframe you need the information in.

Data analysis

Once you have feedback from other people and your own assessment of your strengths, you can now analyse the data for key themes and patterns. You may find it helpful to create a table of common themes.

Theme	Example	Who Noticed?	Comments

These themes will help you build a picture of how you create value in the world and how you impact other people.

Create a summary of your strengths

Take the information you have gleaned from your own analysis and the feedback you have received from others to compile your list of key strengths.

Now review this list of strengths and ask yourself: "Do I want to continue using this strength?"

Just because you are good at something doesn't mean you enjoy doing it!! Or perhaps you have over-used that strength in the past and now want to expand on other strengths that you have.

Once you have done this, you will have the list of strengths that you want to leverage in your future Career Vision.

Considering Your Aspirations for Development

Your aspirations for development are also a major factor in determining what your version of career success looks like. Before you start planning ahead, spend a few moments reflecting on your progress so far.

To do this, return to your Career Timeline and add in more details around key milestones. Not simply the jobs you have done and the skills and strengths you used to do them, but the standout moments in terms of success and achievements. This could be promotion points or when you gained professional qualifications. It could also be informal milestones. For example, when you felt like you had truly mastered a new skill or performed well on a particular piece of work.

When you do this, again, take a moment to reflect on how far you have come already. We often brush off our achievements and take them for granted, but it's important to take a moment to acknowledge them. Then, look ahead to the future and ask yourself:

- How would I like to continue to develop in my career?
- What does that look like specifically? For example, qualifications, courses, skill development, industry experience?
- What resources do I need to help me to develop?
- How can I make a contribution and support others with their career development?

This final question is incredibly important. We want to create a working world that allows us to come up with our own definition of success. If we want the cooperation and support of others to bring our version of a successful career to life, it's important that we do that for others in turn. So, as we grow and progress in our careers, we'll need to be mindful of how we can help those coming up the ladder – or travelling along the squiggle, to use the squiggly careers analogy – behind us.

Articulating Your Career Vision

Taking into consideration your ideal day, your financial aspirations, your strengths, and your development aspirations, ask yourself again: "What does career success look like to me?"

As you clarify your Career Vision, you must find a way to articulate that vision. Stephen Covey shared the importance of "beginning with the end in mind" in his book *The 7 Habits of Highly Effective People*.[8] In other words, before you crack on doing the doing, you need to be super clear on where you are trying to go.

A vision board, used properly, can be the perfect representation of the end that you have in mind. You may have seen vision boards before. My suggestion to create your own might be met with scepticism. I completely understand! I was born and grew up on the west coast of Scotland. As a result, I'm a confirmed realist. I, too, was sceptical about the value of vision boards when I first heard of them. Creating pretty pictures of my dream life and career sounded like a waste of time. However, once I learned there was science behind it, I was hooked...

How Your Brain Can Help You Get What You Want

The brain is exceptionally powerful. Our reticular activating system is a spectacular part of the brain that helps us get what we want. The brain stores hundreds of thousands of pieces of information at all times, but we do not use all of the information at the same time. For example, the seven times table is firmly lodged in your brain and probably has been for some years. Your reticular activating system only fires up when somebody asks you: "What is seven times seven?" Then, your brain focuses on that specific fact and brings that information to the front of your mind.

Your body breathes 24 hours a day, 7 days a week. You don't have to think about it. Your brain is constantly sending the signal to your body to breathe. It's only when I say to you "focus on your breath" that you notice that you are breathing.

Our brains are designed to conserve energy and so they only focus on things when they need to. Otherwise, just like your phone or laptop, it goes to sleep. It does the minimum required when not needed for a particular task. Our cave people ancestors were primarily focused on finding food and staying alive. They had to conserve their energy and attention to make sure there was enough left to focus on finding their next meal and fend off predators.

In the modern world, the threat to life is not quite so imminent but generally our brains focus on two things:

- Dealing with threats in our environment and emergencies as they arise.
- Achieving the goals that are important to our happiness, wellbeing, and overall satisfaction.

A very simple example of the reticular activating system acting to help you achieve a goal is when you decide to make a specific purchase. Suddenly you start to notice that item everywhere you go. You have conversations with people who have just or are about to purchase the same or a very similar item.

A few years ago, we had a new kitchen installed. We had lived in our local area for eight years. Yet all of a sudden, I started to notice kitchen showrooms and other related shops everywhere I went. I would chat with friends and notice how many of them were also refurbishing their kitchens at the same time. The word 'kitchen' automatically aroused my brain. I had indicated that this was important to me. As a result, discount codes and advertising materials relating to kitchen showrooms were jumping out at me. My brain was focused on bringing my new kitchen to life. It opened my eyes and ears to everything in my environment that could support me to achieve that goal.

By articulating your vision and creating a vision board in a clear, meaningful, and succinct way, you are telling your reticular activating system that your Career Vision is important. If you place that vision board somewhere you will see it every day, this will remind your brain of what is important to you. Your brain then takes action. It starts to seek opportunities to help bring that vision to life.

Create a Vision Board

You can choose how you create your vision board. The most important thing is that it is meaningful to you. When you look at it, you should feel inspired. You might decide to:

- Create a collage of images using online resources and magazines
- Set up a digital vision board using a tool such as Pinterest or Trello
- Design a digital collage using a tool such as Canva or Picmonkey
- Draw your vision
- Collate a list of phrases that encapsulate your vision

Vision Boards in Action

Nigel was deeply unhappy at work. He was working in a toxic environment and dreaded going to work. Nigel engaged with me to define his exit strategy and identify what he wanted to do next with his career. For financial reasons, Nigel needed to stay in his current role for another 12 months and had made peace with that. He was willing to tolerate a less-than-perfect work environment for the financial reward he knew was coming his way.

I encouraged Nigel to create a vision board of the life he wanted for himself. He made a wonderful digital collage that articulated what he wanted from his professional and personal life. He found this a great tool to keep him focused and motivated. He used it as he navigated a difficult year and finished up in his role.

Having clarity on what he wanted helped him to bring more of it into his current reality. Spending time in nature was important to him. While he couldn't embark on a career where he spent most of his day outside, he committed to daily walks and spent more time in his garden.

Once you've made your vision board for your Career Vision, remember it's a live document. You may want to change or tweak it as time goes on. Don't create it and forget it. Use it as a catalyst to encourage you to take action to bring your Career Vision to life every single day. Staring at your vision board is not going to create the career or life you want. However, you can use it as tool to stay focused and inspire you to take action. Doing the work is how you get the career or life you want.

In a Nutshell

- Your Career Vision is your big picture. It is what you are working towards and what you want to have more of in your life and career.
- Your Career Vision needs to align with your current season of life and reflect the time, energy, and attention you have available to devote to your career.
- Career success means different things to different people. To help you define your version of career success: map out your ideal day; understand your financial motivations, know your strengths and how you want to use your strengths at work; consider how you want to grow and develop in the future.
- Use a vision board to articulate your vision and encapsulate what you want from your career.
- Once you articulate your Career Vision, the reticular activating system in your brain will help you to seek out opportunities to bring your vision to life.

Chapter 5

Your Career Goals

"In the absence of clearly defined goals, we become strangely loyal to performing daily acts of trivia."

Robert Heinlein

Your Career Goals are the specific milestones that you want to achieve on your journey to bringing your Career Vision to life. Your Career Goals can either be long-term or short-term. Given the ever-changing nature of the world we live in, I would recommend setting Career Goals for the next 12-18 months. This gives you enough time to achieve something meaningful, without committing yourself for too long.

Once you're clear about your goals, you can take purposeful action to achieve them. No more drifting, no more going with the flow, no more doing what other people want you to do because you're unsure of what you want. As you act on what's important to you, you build momentum. Building momentum leads to results, and results grow your sense of self-worth and achievement. Sounds good, doesn't it?

Why is Goal Setting Important?

In the book *What They Don't Teach You at Harvard Business School*, Mark McCormack, an American lawyer, sports agent, and writer, talks about a study conducted on students in the 1979 Harvard MBA Programme.[9]

In that year, the students were asked: "Have you set clear, written goals for your future and made plans to accomplish them?"

Only 3% of graduates had written goals and plans. A further 13% had goals but not in writing. A massive 84% had no specific goals.

Ten years later, the members of the class were interviewed again. The findings were incredible. The 13% of the class who had goals were earning, on average, twice as much as the 84% who had no goals at all. And the 3% who had clear, written goals were earning, on average, ten times as much as the other 97% put together.

This is no coincidence. The 3% that had written down their goals had focused on **what they wanted** and worked out exactly **what they had to do** to be successful. Financial goals are not the be all and end all. However, this is an excellent example of how setting goals can deliver results.

Many of my clients are reluctant to set goals. They have been burned and bruised from their appraisal system at work. Perhaps they have been forced to set incredibly ambitious, unachievable goals. They feel like they are set up to fail before they even get started. Or perhaps they see goal setting as an academic exercise, purely for their performance review. They don't see it as a powerful tool that can help them get what they want.

What Happens in Your Brain When You Set Goals?

Building on what we already discussed about the reticular activating system in Chapter 4, when you create Career Goals, this gives your brain a set of even more sophisticated filters. It sifts information in your environment through these filters. For example, one element of your Career Vision could be to become known as a speaker within your industry. If you set a goal to speak at three events in the UK within the next year, your brain can start to spot opportunities to help you achieve that goal. You move from aspiration to specifics.

One key factor that prevents us from staying focused on our goals and achieving them is that it's hard to direct our attention on them all the time or often enough. There are so many distractions and demands in our everyday life. It seems almost impossible to stay focused.

If you have no goals or you haven't clearly articulated your goals, your brain is going to go into 'sleep mode'. If you don't have a plan in place to achieve those goals, the same happens. Your brain will only react to what is being asked of it. It won't constantly scan the environment for opportunities to bring those goals to life. Without passion and enthusiasm for specific goals, your brain will not recognise the opportunities, resources, or people that could support you in making them happen.

On the other hand, when you have clear, specific goals, your reticular activating system helps you pay attention. They make it easier to get and stay focused. When you write down your goals, you get specific about what you want to bring into your life. This includes achievements, experiences, people, places, emotions, feelings, and more. You get crystal clear on exactly what you want.

As you do this, your reticular activating system is aroused and puts you on alert, ready to respond to cues in the environment that are relevant to your goals. When the reticular activating system is activated, you can process and reorganise information much more efficiently.

For example, you set the goal that you want to speak at three events related to your industry in the next 12 months. Then:

- You notice an 'Improve Your Public Speaking' course advertised on your company intranet.
- You see posts on LinkedIn about events that people in your network are attending. This leads you to connect with the organisers of those events.
- You tell friends and colleagues about your goal. They spot opportunities on your behalf and send details to you.

None of these things are a coincidence. Now that you've set the goal of speaking at events, your reticular activating system is helping you notice things in your environment – things that are already there and you just haven't noticed before – that will help you be successful.

What Do You Want?

To help you identify your specific Career Goals, go back, and look at your Career Vision. Think about the steps you need to take in the next 12-18 months to bring that Career Vision to life.

Your Career Vision may seem daunting at the moment. You might wonder how you'll achieve the great things you've identified for yourself. But how do you eat an elephant? You break it down and eat it one bite at a time. This is exactly what you are doing with your Career Vision. You are going to take elements of that Career Vision and break them down into bite-sized chunks, creating specific Career Goals. You can work on these chunks over the next 12-18 months. You don't need to do it all at once; just what is manageable for you in that period of time.

When you have all your potential goals written down, it's time to sift through them. You won't have the time, energy, or attention to work on all of them. We know that if we try to take on too much and spread ourselves too thin, we won't successfully achieve any of our goals.

Here are some filters that you can use to check your goals and see which ones are most compelling for you.

1. How do you feel when you read the goal?

When you read the goal, do you feel excited and enthused? Or do you feel like it is something that you should do rather than something that lights you up? Cross off any of the 'shoulds' from your list.

I have completed a number of walking marathons in recent years. There's a little voice in the back of my head that says: *"Wouldn't it be cool to run a marathon?"* That seems like the next natural step. The thing is I don't enjoy running. At all. And I'm not very good at it. In fact, when I pick up the pace, I can walk faster than I can run. While I often feel like I 'should' add 'run a marathon' to my list of goals, in my heart of hearts it doesn't excite me.

2. Do you want to do the work required to achieve this goal?

It's one thing to set yourself a lofty goal, but if you know that you are never going to do the work then be honest about it. Going back to that marathon example (and ignoring for now that I don't like running!), I would need to ask myself: "Do I want to commit to a six-month training plan to run a marathon?" Translated, this means considering whether I want to adjust my social life to fit in my training or change my diet to get the nutrition I need to sustain me through training, and so on.

You've got to be honest. If you're not honest, all you will do is set yourself up for failure. You will commit to goals that you are never going to achieve. You will not be prepared to put in the work to get the results that you say that you want. It's far better to be honest with yourself. Don't set yourself up with unrealistic expectations.

Now that you've taken the 'shoulds' and the 'can't be bothered enoughs' off your list, you will start to narrow down your goals.

3. Does the goal align with your Career Values?

You can use your values to sense-check your priorities and goals. If your highest value is work-life balance, setting a goal to 'secure a role in the global team' may not align with that. This type of role will require travel. It will also involve online meetings early in the morning and late at night to accommodate different time zones. Work your way through your potential goals and check in with whether they align with your values, again, if they don't, score them off the list.

You should now be left with a small but perfectly formed list. At this point, we want to reduce it even further. This is where a lot of people go wrong with goal setting. They try to do too many things. They have good intentions, but they don't have enough time or energy to do all the things. They spread themselves too thin, get frustrated, and end up giving up. They don't achieve any of them.

I want to encourage you to choose a maximum of three goals. Researchers have debated the maximum number of items we can store in our conscious mind. This is called our working memory. A study published by Cambridge University[10] puts the limit at three or four.

It might feel uncomfortable to limit yourself to three goals. It may feel like you are closing the door on opportunities that you want to pursue, but you can reframe this. It's not that you will never pursue those goals; you're just not pursuing them yet. By putting those goals on the backburner for now, you significantly increase your chances of succeeding with the goals you have chosen to pursue.

I have a Japanese peony bush in my garden, which is my symbol of resilience. It has been uprooted and moved several times. The soil conditions are not great, and it's being cared for by someone who is anything but green-fingered. In the early days of having the plant, I was delighted by how quickly it grew. I left it untended until a friend told me that to get the most from the bush, I had to prune it back. By pruning it back, I was making sure the plant's resources – its water and nutrients – were being directed in the most effective way. This allowed the stronger parts of the plant to grow and flourish, while not wasting energy on the weaker parts. And this is exactly what you are doing when you pare down your goals, making way for the best ones to come to fruition.

4. Are your goals SMART?

Please don't slam the book closed!!! I am sure you have heard about SMART goals a million times before. Probably as part of a badly constructed corporate appraisal system. It may bring back memories of goal setting as a box-ticking exercise.

However, while I do think there is merit in running your goal through a check to see if it is SMART, I'd encourage you to go further and check that it is SMARTER.

Specific – If you don't know what you are trying to achieve, how will you know when you get there? 'I want to be appreciated' is vague. 'I want a pay rise' is specific. 'I want to earn £20k more per year' is even more specific and makes it easy to track progress against the goal.

Meaningful – If you've already validated your goal against your values then it should be meaningful, but it is still worth checking. Why are you setting this goal? What makes it important to you? It's the meaning behind the goal that is going to drive you forward to take action.

Achievable – Let's not set ourselves up for failure. We've already asked ourselves if we are willing to do the work to achieve the goal. Once you have made the goal specific, make sure it is still achievable. Maybe wanting to earn an extra £20k per annum is achievable for you, but it's highly unlikely that you would make an extra £200k a year, for example.

Relevant – Are the goals relevant for you and your stage of life? Think back to that example of the new parent whose highest value was family. Would taking on the International Sales Manager role, which involves lots of travel, be relevant at this stage of life? Probably not. On the other hand, let's say you worked part-time while an elderly parent recuperated from a hip replacement and now, they're fully mobile and independent again. You may have the capacity for a new challenge, so a goal of completing an accreditation or doing some professional development is likely to be relevant right now.

Time Bound – This is simply setting yourself a deadline, which helps to make your goal measurable and also allows you to hold yourself to account. This doesn't need to be complicated: 'I will earn an extra £20k per annum by the end of 2025.'

Now, I did say I want you to make your goals SMARTER not just SMART.

The E stands for **Evaluate**. Once you start to work on your goal, you might find that it no longer holds the same appeal, becomes unimportant or less relevant for you. In which case you don't want to just carry on regardless, working on something because you said you would. Evaluating your goals regularly keeps them top of mind. They won't become something you wrote down months ago and never look at again. They are real, they are live, and you are tracking your progress against them. By building in this evaluation, you are automatically creating a mechanism to hold yourself accountable.

And finally, the R is for **Readjust**. You might need to change your goal if it no longer feels right for you. Or you might need to adjust the actions you take to achieve your goal. This is based on your progress and what you've learned so far.

5. What's stopping you from being successful?

Forewarned is forearmed. What obstacles could potentially get in the way of you achieving your goals? Knowing the possible barriers so that you can spot them as they arise is powerful. You can work out your mitigation strategies to overcome any challenges and keep you on track.

Caroline wanted to return to a client-facing consulting role, having spent a considerable amount of time on secondment as Chief of Staff to the Head of Advisory. It was only ever meant to be a 12-month secondment, but she found herself in the same role nearly four years later. To a certain extent, Caroline was a victim of her own success. She had done such a good job in the role that the Head of Advisory was reluctant to let her go. He knew that it would take a while for somebody else to climb the steep learning curve to be able to carry out the role efficiently and effectively.

When I asked Caroline what was going to stop her from successfully making the transition, she identified three things. The first was convincing the Head of Advisory to let her go. This turned out to be quite straightforward. He didn't want Caroline to move on. However, he could appreciate that it was the right thing for her career progression. The second was securing a role back in a client-facing position. Again, this was more straightforward than Caroline anticipated too. She was quickly assigned to a new client and given responsibility to grow the account. The third thing that Caroline identified was her! She wanted to transition back to being client-facing. However, she knew she would find it hard to leave her current role. She had worked hard to set up processes and systems. She had built incredible relationships. She was concerned about the impact a new person would have on those relationships. Ultimately, she didn't believe that anybody could do the job as well as she could.

Armed with this knowledge, Caroline was able to question some of her behaviour and decisions. When she was interviewing for a replacement, she had been hyper-critical. She had to stop herself from telling the Head of Advisory that there were no suitable candidates. She heard about a new restructuring project that was about to launch and resisted the temptation of saying she would extend her secondment by another six months to see it through. Caroline had to accept that no time would be a good time to leave her role. She had to let go. While it would take her replacement time to get up to speed, the organisation would not grind to a halt when she moved on.

Are You Setting Big Hairy Audacious Goals?

In their book *Built to Last*, Jim Collins and Jerry Porras[11] talked about compelling long-term goals or big hairy audacious goals that inspire employees to take action. The purpose of BHAGs was to get people energised and motivated to work towards a goal over a longer timeframe. In recent years, the BHAG idea has been used more generally when talking about goal setting.

Many times, I have been encouraged to set BHAGs for my own life and career. When I worked in corporate, I worked for some of the biggest organisations in the world. The scale at which we operated and the collective impact of everyone in each of those organisations was immense. When I branched out and became self-employed, I couldn't operate at that scale or have that level of impact anymore. To begin with, it felt incredibly uncomfortable! Was I wasting my education and experience? Was I not fulfilling my potential because I could no longer have such a large impact?

The Dalai Lama said: *"If you think you are too small to make a difference, try sleeping with a mosquito."* It doesn't take much to imagine what it's like being trapped in a small, enclosed space with a mosquito... and the discomfort you feel when you wake up the next day to discover you are covered in hot, red, itchy bites. Depending on where you are in the world, that mosquito could even be carrying some deadly diseases. So, while it is teeny tiny, it can have a massive and not altogether positive impact.

If you consider yourself in the role of the mosquito, what are the things that you do in your career that have a wider impact and implication than you might first think?

I did some pro bono work with an incredible young woman. She wanted to be promoted to Senior Receptionist in her organisation. In that role, she would be leading a team of two. To the outside world, that might not seem like a BHAG. Why is she only aspiring to lead a team of two? Why doesn't she work for a bigger organisation and lead a team of 10 or even 20? However, this woman was cripplingly shy at school. When she was younger, she could not bring herself to talk to strangers. As a receptionist, she is the first port of call when a person comes into the building. She sets the tone and gives the initial impression of the organisation, so the way that she interacts with people has a huge impact. Over the years, her confidence had grown, and she was good at her job. Now, she felt capable of taking on a Senior Receptionist role. While her goal might not seem like a BHAG to the outside world, it most certainly was for her.

There was a time when working for a big organisation was seen as the way to make an impact in the world. The idea that bigger is better! I think people are increasingly realising there are many benefits to working for a smaller organisation and making an impact is still possible.

One of my neighbours set up a small charity called Meals for More. The ethos is very simple. They connect people in the local community who are willing to donate either cooked meals or groceries to those who need short-term additional support. Each month, Meals for More supports around 100 families. This is tiny compared to the work done by some of the big global charities. But it makes a massive difference for those 100 families.

One story that demonstrates the impact of Meals for More is that of a young person living alone who was delivered his first meal package. He had been applying for jobs and going for interviews but hadn't had any luck so far. After getting his meal package, he fed himself a good breakfast. Then, he went for an interview and got the job. He was convinced that he had been successful because he hadn't gone to the interview hungry and was able to concentrate. Something as simple as being able to have a good breakfast had a massive impact on his life.

I encourage you to think about your goals and actions. Consider the wider impact you are having. Your goals don't necessarily need to be big or bold or even particularly visible to other people. Your contribution, whatever the size, can be enough to make an impact.

In a Nutshell

- Setting Career Goals helps you to direct your time, energy, and attention to the milestones you want to focus on to bring your Career Vision to life.
- To define your Career Goals: ask yourself what you want to focus on and then identify the things that you find exciting and compelling. It's important to remember to check whether you are actually willing to do the work required to achieve the goal, as well as checking that the potential goals align with your values.
- Don't set too many goals at once. Narrow your goals down to a maximum of three.
- Make your goals SMARTER - Specific, Meaningful, Achievable, Relevant, Timebound - and then be sure to Evaluate and Readjust. Know what might stop you from being successful and create your mitigation strategies.
- Remember that you don't need to set big hairy audacious goals. Your contribution, whatever the size, can make a big impact.

Chapter 6

Your Career Beliefs

"You are what you believe yourself to be."

Paulo Coelho

You have probably heard the Henry Ford quote, "whether you think you can, or you can't, you're right". It is so over-used in social media posts that it feels cliché to share it here, but it's true! What we believe about ourselves will in large part influence how confident we feel about navigating our career and ultimately determine our career success.

Our beliefs are what we understand to be true. They form the lens through which we see the world and perceive reality. We assume our beliefs are true, regardless of whether we have evidence to back them up. They act as a filter that influences how we interpret information and events. These interpretations shape our emotions, thoughts, and behaviours. Two people faced with the same circumstances can have completely different reactions to the same situation due to their belief system. For example, Jack believes he can achieve anything he sets his mind to, approaches challenges with optimism and enthusiasm, takes a proactive approach and gets stuck in. Meanwhile, John has a more pessimistic belief system. When faced with challenges, he gets himself into a spin, convinces himself he won't be successful and then struggles to take action.

Your Career Beliefs are the things that you believe to be true about you and your ability to navigate your career. Your Career Beliefs can either help or hinder you to be successful in your career. Take for example your beliefs about financial reward. Some people believe that money comes to them easily and effortlessly. They believe they deserve to be paid well for the work they do. Other people believe that it's greedy to expect to be paid more for the work they do, and they should be satisfied with what they have. Your belief systems about money will largely influence your salary expectations, which will also affect how you approach pay negotiations.

How Are Beliefs Formed?

As humans, we need to make sense of the world around us. From a young age, we are wired to look for patterns and connections. This helps us create a framework to navigate the complexities of life. These patterns and connections lay the foundation for our beliefs. Our brains then scan our environment and identify information that fits neatly into the frameworks they have created.

As a young child, your beliefs had not yet formed. When you were learning to walk, you would hold onto the table, pull yourself up, attempt to take a few steps and fall over. Then you'd haul yourself up and try again. You didn't fall over once and decide: *"Oh, that's it. I'm not cut out for this walking malarkey. I'm not even going to bother trying."* You didn't look at all the other kids in the playgroup and say to yourself: *"My tower of bricks isn't as tall as theirs."* You also didn't think: *"That girl is rocking the nappy in tights look so much better than I ever could!"* When we were toddlers, we didn't care what others thought about us. We strutted around in our mismatched outfits with the remains of our breakfast around our faces. We thought we were the bee's knees. We were shining beacons of inner confidence.

Most of our core beliefs are formed when we are children between the ages of 0-7, when our brains are like sponges, soaking in everything from the environment around us. During this time, we formed neural pathways, which guide our decisions and behaviour for the rest of our life. Our beliefs continue to develop and evolve over our lifetime, fuelled by our experiences, cultural background, the society we live in and the opinions of important people in our life.

Our Experiences

Personal experiences play a pivotal role in shaping our beliefs. Our encounters with the world, whether positive or negative, make an impact and shape our perspectives. If a person grows up surrounded by love and kindness, they may develop a belief that people are inherently good. On the flip side, if a person experiences hurt and deceit, they may be cynical and not trust others. Our experiences in childhood heavily shape what we believe as adults. Even seemingly innocuous events can have a long-lasting impact.

Debra is in a Senior Manager role at a large accountancy firm. She is ambitious, very highly regarded, and well-liked by her team members and clients. She is eager to be promoted to Director. However, she knows she must participate in presentations and sales pitches to new clients to be successful in this role. When Debra participates in client presentations, she puts in hours of preparation. She knows she doesn't need to spend so much time preparing. However, it's the only way she can feel comfortable presenting to an audience. She is concerned that taking on a Director role and the need to participate in more presentations will lead to an unsustainable workload.

When Debra was in her final year of primary school, she had a small role in her end of year performance. On the day of the performance, the girl who was cast as the lead character was unwell. Debra was asked to step into the role of the lead character at the last minute. She was terrified throughout the entire performance and forgot some of her lines. From that point forward, Debra vowed that if she ever stood up in front of an audience, she would prepare for every possibility and never leave anything to chance. Debra's experience at primary school is the root cause of her decision to not pursue promotion and step into a role she is more than capable of doing.

The People Around Us

The people around us greatly influence the beliefs we form. Your family, friends, and teachers all contribute to the beliefs you hold. When we are very young, we can't discern between what is true and false. We accept what we are told as truth and those stories build up into beliefs. If you were always the last person to get picked for a team in your P.E. class, this could lead to a lifelong belief that you are not sporty. On the other hand, if your P.E. teacher allocated people to teams randomly and praised everyone for their effort not their results, you are more likely to believe that you can give any sport a go, even if you are not the best at it.

Suzanne was a bright, academic child. Her parents encouraged her to work hard and pursue her studies. There wasn't much time left for anything else. Her childhood was split between school, homework, and practicing and preparing for piano exams. Suzanne started working for a Private Equity firm when she graduated from university. She rapidly rose through the ranks and eventually was made Partner. Suzanne works long hours and rarely takes time off. She is on the brink of burnout. However, she is struggling to step away from work to give herself the time and space she needs to recover. She believes that working intensely for long hours is a prerequisite for success.

Culture and Upbringing

The culture you are brought up in is an invisible force shaping the way you see the world. Whether it's the traditions passed down through the generations or the food you grow up eating, they form the bedrock of who you are and what is important to you. If you grew up in the UK, Christmas without a turkey and brussels sprouts is unimaginable. But if you are of Portuguese heritage, you will be celebrating the day with salt cod and boiled potatoes. Cultural norms relating to working hours, work ethic and family expectations will influence your approach to your career.

Charles was born and brought up in London, the son of first-generation immigrants from India. Growing up, Charles was taught to value education above all else. His parents made a modest living, but they invested their money in a private school education for Charles and his two sisters. Charles graduated from university with a law degree and secured a training contract with a prestigious City firm. His parents were over the moon. Charles pursued a career in law for nearly a decade but never felt passionate about it.

As he approached his 30th birthday, Charles found himself despondent and deeply unhappy. When I asked him what he would do if he could pursue any job, regardless of salary expectations, he said he wanted to be a gardener. He loves working in nature and desperately wanted to follow an alternative career path. However, his conditioning and upbringing made it incredibly difficult for him to believe it was acceptable to follow his dream.

The Society We Live In

Societal influences also contribute to our beliefs. We are social creatures. Our ideas are often shaped by the norms and values of the communities to which we belong. Our experiences of education, the media, politics, and social media introduce and reinforce our beliefs. In many cases, it is a subtle process. We adopt the beliefs of those around us without even questioning them.

According to a survey by Resume Builder, over three-quarters of Gen Zers say that they regularly get career advice from TikTok and 41% of Gen Zers have made career decisions based on information they have found on the site.[12] Often without even realising, people are adopting the beliefs of people they know online. Before social media, new entrants to the workforce would seek advice from co-workers, mentors, and others with experience in their company, industry, and profession. Now they get advice from people they follow on TikTok, who may have no direct experience of their career circumstances.

Our beliefs are a patchwork quilt of our experience, culture, personal interpretation, and the persuasive powers of those around us. They are the stories we tell ourselves about the world.

How Our Beliefs Impact Our Career

The beliefs we hold about ourselves can either be supportive or limiting. Supportive beliefs will help boost our confidence. They will also help us to feel competent, capable, and in control of our working lives. Supportive beliefs are things like:

- I have the skills and experience that I need to be successful in this role.
- I am a valued member of my team, and my contribution helps us achieve our collective goals.
- I can confidently communicate and adapt my style as required.
- I am resilient in the face of setbacks.
- I am adaptable and can lead my team through times of change and transition.

Limiting beliefs are thoughts that hold us back. They lead us to question our abilities and have a detrimental impact on our confidence. Common limiting beliefs about our career are:

- I'm not qualified enough to do that job.
- People like me don't work in a place like that.
- There is no point in me speaking up, since people don't listen to what I have to say.
- Other people are so much more productive/effective/intelligent/qualified than me.

- I've tried to be more assertive, but people just don't listen to me.

When expressing limiting beliefs, they usually begin with one of the following phrases:

- I can't
- I don't
- I'm not
- I've tried… and it hasn't worked
- It's too late
- They're better
- I don't deserve
- I've been told

What Do You Believe to Be True In Relation to Your Career?

Have a look back over the milestones or highlights that you added to your Career Timeline. Thinking of these achievements, answer this question:

- What positive, supportive beliefs do you hold about yourself concerning your career?

Now notice some of the lower points in your career when you didn't feel like you were getting where you wanted to go. Make a list now:

- What limiting beliefs do you hold about yourself concerning your career?

Take time to reflect on what has led you to believe these supporting and limiting beliefs. For each of those you've written down, identify examples or patterns:

- What experiences, people, or influences have led you to form that belief?

The good news is that our beliefs are not set in stone. We can choose to change our beliefs and our thoughts so that our reality shifts to become exactly what we want it to be. As Mahatma Gandhi said: *"A man (or a woman!) is but the product of his thoughts. What he thinks, he becomes."* We can build our Career Confidence by continually reinforcing the supportive beliefs that we hold. We can also build confidence by changing the beliefs that hold us back.

You may be thinking: *"Wait a minute, I've held these beliefs my whole life. How on earth can I change them?"* The good news is that the human brain is incredibly powerful and has the ability to rewire itself. This process is known as "neuroplasticity", which describes the capacity of our brain cells to change in response to our behaviour.

The brain's neural pathways formed in childhood are reinforced by your life experiences. Our beliefs are essentially neural pathways that the brain creates. The more you repeat and practice an action, the stronger the neural pathway becomes. Imagine your brain is a forest. The well-trodden signposted paths in the forest are your beliefs. They are familiar to you and are often your autopilot response. If you want to create a new belief, you need to create a new pathway in the forest. At first, it can be difficult as you navigate your way through the overgrown weeds and patches of mud. After you've trodden along the pathway for a while, the route becomes easier, and you need to put in much less effort to find your way. If you want to change your beliefs, you need to stop walking down the same old pathways and start to forge a new path for yourself. The more often you take that path, the clearer it becomes.

How to Change Your Beliefs

The American self-development author Byron Katie[13] developed a simple set of questions to help shift beliefs and start forming new neural pathways. When you notice the voice in your head tell you something negative, ask yourself:

- Is that true?
- Is it absolutely true?
- What happens when I believe that thought?
- Who would I be without that thought?
- What will I believe instead?

I encourage you to become your own personal private detective. Notice your thoughts and the beliefs you hold about yourself. Challenge yourself and ask if those thoughts are true or a story you tell yourself.

I liken this process to peeling back the layers of an onion. You work through layer by layer. You shed the unhelpful thoughts and beliefs that have been holding you back from achieving your goals. As you shed each layer of unhelpful beliefs, you become a smaller, shinier onion. Perhaps those outer layers have kept you safe in the past, but you no longer need them.

Belief Change in Action

Maria was feeling frustrated. Her manager was leaving the organisation and Maria was certain that one of her colleagues Christine, who had been in the team for nearly 10 years, would be appointed as the new Head of Department. While Maria got on well with Christine, they had very different outlooks and disagreed on the extent the team should get involved with cross-functional projects. Maria was concerned that she would have limited access to interesting work and development opportunities with Christine at the helm. When I asked Maria why she didn't apply for the Head of Department role, her response was: "It's a big promotion. I'm not experienced enough to go for it."

I encouraged Maria to challenge her thinking. I asked her: "Is it true that you are not experienced enough?" Her initial response was: "Of course it's true." She had only been with the organisation for two years. Her colleague had been there for over ten.

I challenged her further and asked: "Is it absolutely true that you are not experienced enough?" That's when Maria began to unravel her thinking. While she had only been with the organisation for two years, she realised she had an additional 12 years of experience in the same industry. During those two most recent years at the firm, she had been involved in a wide range of projects and consistently received excellent feedback.

Then I asked Maria: "What happens when you believe that you are not experienced enough?" Her answer was enlightening! She realised that telling herself she wasn't experienced enough made her feel relieved. She wouldn't have to face the disappointment of not getting the job if she wasn't successful. If she told herself she wasn't experienced enough, she wouldn't need to step into the pressure of a more senior role. She also wouldn't need to navigate the transition from being a colleague to a manager.

I asked Maria how she would feel and what she would do if she did believe she was experienced enough to apply for the job. She realised that she would feel excited about the possibility of stepping into the Head of Department role. She would feel confident that she had the skills and abilities required to be successful. While she didn't relish the prospect of navigating difficult relationships with her current colleagues, she knew she could if she had to do so.

With this newfound sense of excitement, I encouraged Maria to think about what she could choose to believe. She decided to change her belief from 'I'm not experienced enough for the role' to 'I have all the skills and experience I need to apply for the promotion'.

This simple set of questions is a powerful way to help you consider any beliefs that are holding you back. It's also a way to reframe those beliefs.

As a side note, Maria applied for the role and was successful. Her colleague didn't even apply for the position. While she had much more experience than Maria, she had no desire to take on the additional responsibility of being Head of Department. An important reminder to never make assumptions about what other people want or what they will do!

With this lesson in mind, go back and review your Career Vision and your Career Goals for the next 12-18 months. What supportive beliefs do you need to develop to bring your vision to life and achieve your goals? What actions can you take to build and reinforce these supportive beliefs?

Gathering Evidence to Reinforce Your Supportive Beliefs

You have been viewing the world through the lens of your limiting beliefs for a very long time. As a result, your mind has gathered evidence to reinforce this belief. Now that you have chosen more positive beliefs to help you achieve your Career Goals, you need to gather evidence to support these beliefs. The more you notice evidence to reinforce the belief, the more it will happen.

This is your reticular activating system in action again. (Don't you just love your reticular activating system?) It's like the game you play with kids to pass the time on a long journey where you spot red cars. Before you start to play the game, there seems to be an even number of different coloured cars on the road. But as soon as you start to focus on red cars, you see them everywhere. You have spent years telling yourself negative stories. You have gathered evidence to support those stories. If you switch to a more helpful and supportive belief, your brain will now gather evidence to support and reinforce that new belief.

When gathering evidence, you'll want to write it down so that you can visually see all the evidence building. You can use this as an excuse to treat yourself to a lovely new notepad and pen or you can even create an online folder. Gather together:

- Extracts from performance reviews
- Messages from satisfied clients/stakeholders
- Positive feedback that you have received

This will give you something tangible to refer to that will remind you of the progress you are making, and reinforce your new positive beliefs.

Be Kind to Yourself

Changing our beliefs doesn't happen overnight. It can be challenging. So, it's important to give ourselves a break, cut ourselves some slack and be kind to ourselves along the way. We tend to be harder on ourselves than we would be on other people. Imagine talking to a friend or colleague the way that you often talk to yourself.

When those feelings of overwhelm and feeling 'less than' hit you, take 30 seconds to show yourself some kindness.

- Breathe in and tell yourself: "I'm doing my best"
- Breathe out and tell yourself: "Let go of the rest"

This short moment of pause and release can have a hugely positive impact on your emotional state.

Conquering Your Inner Critic

Your inner critic is the little voice in our heads that tells us we are 'not good enough', 'not intelligent enough', 'not pretty enough'... basically 'not enough'. Our inner critic articulates the limiting beliefs we hold about ourselves. We've all got one and it tends to get vocal when we embark on something new or when we stretch ourselves outside of our comfort zone.

- If you are in a meeting and you make a point that others don't agree with, it's the voice in your head that says: *"Well, that was stupid. I'll just keep quiet from now on."*

- If you are considering a career move, your inner critic might tell you: "You're lucky to have the job that you're in. Don't rock the boat. You're not qualified to do anything else."

- If you think about volunteering for a cross-functional project, it might say: *"Wait a minute, missy. Do you realise you'll have to work much longer hours? Just stick to what you know. You probably wouldn't get invited onto the project team anyway."*

Your inner critic might seem unhelpful; however, its main job is to keep you safe. It's the part of yourself that doesn't want you to face discomfort or disappointment, so it's protecting you from harm. The world can be a scary place and we are always alert to danger. In prehistoric days, that danger presented itself in the form of predators that could cause us physical harm. In our modern world, the risk of predators coming and gobbling us up is slim. However, our brains are still wired to protect us from danger.

The voice of our inner critic is one of the tools in our repertoire to keep us safe from perceived harm. You go into autopilot mode and use past experience to predict future situations. To illustrate this, imagine touching a hot fire. Your automatic reaction is to move your hand away from a fire. If you had to think it through logically and process what is happening, you would probably end up burning your hand. By the time your logical thought process worked out what you needed to do, your hand would have been on the fire for too long. Our inner critic works in a similar way. When our brain perceives us to be doing something new (e.g. a career move) or putting ourselves at risk (e.g. speaking up in a meeting), our inner critic steps in to keep us safe. Unfortunately, it can keep us so safe that it stops us from taking any risks at all, including the action required to achieve the goals that we set ourselves.

How to Take Control of Your Inner Critic

1. Get familiar

There will likely be a pattern of negative self-talk behind your inner critic. It's not possible to 'turn off' the voice of your inner critic. Your inner critic's voice has developed over many years based on your past experiences. It reflects the feedback you've received from others and your perceptions of this feedback. It will always be there in the background. Listen to what the voice is saying to you. What can you learn from it?

That said, you don't need to believe everything your inner critic tells you. It's a voice. It is not the truth. When you recognise your inner critic, respond thoughtfully and rationally. Don't let emotions take over.

For example, you are sitting in a team meeting and your manager is looking for somebody to take on a new project. You know that you are already overloaded, but the voice in your head says: *"You're letting the team down. Somebody has to do it. Come on, you need to say yes to this. She's looking at you. She thinks you're lazy because you haven't already volunteered."*

If you immediately react to your inner critic, you will have another project to add to your busy workload. You might feel growing resentment. You are always the one volunteering for these things. However, if you can allow yourself a few moments to recognise that your inner critic has taken over, you can have a rational internal conversation. Then, you will be able to acknowledge that:

- You already have too much on your plate.

- You would be doing your manager a disservice to say yes.
- You wouldn't be able to give the project the time, energy, and attention it requires.

While you have been working through these thoughts, a more junior team member has volunteered. They have more time available. Plus, it will be a great development opportunity for them. It's a win-win.

Once you've been noticing your inner critic's voice for a while, take some time to note down any patterns:

- What are the repeated stories that your inner critic tells you?
- When your inner critic starts to tell you these stories, what is your default 'autopilot' response?

2. Give your inner critic its own identity

As you get better at recognising when your inner critic starts talking, you might want to give it an identity. Creating a persona for your inner critic can dampen the emotion you feel when those thoughts kick in.

My inner critic is called Doris. A few years ago, I bought a plant pot that has the face of a woman with pursed lips and eyes closed. When I saw the plant pot in the shop, it immediately appealed to me, but it was only when I got it home that I realised she was a visual representation of Doris. In my mind, the look on her face represents: *"Oh Nicola, what kind of nonsense are you thinking of now?"*

When my Doris thoughts start to kick in, I just need to think about the face on that plant pot. I still listen to what Doris has to say to me. However, I can also appreciate that it's slightly ridiculous to listen to what a plant pot is telling me. These thoughts that I am having are just Doris's opinions. They are not truth or fact. Just thoughts.

3. *Notice when your inner critic is active and ask what you need*

As you become more familiar with recognising your inner critic, notice not just what it's telling you, but also *when* that voice emerges. Does your inner critic come out to play more when you are tired? Or when you have been working longer hours? Or when you are trying to multitask and combine work and home time?

What patterns can you notice? And, most importantly, what action do you need to take to help you manage your inner critic?

- Do you need to make sure that you get a certain amount of sleep?
- Do you need to prioritise eating at regular intervals?
- Do you need to have clear boundaries between your work and home life?

By acknowledging and giving yourself what you need, you will build emotional resilience and develop your ability to manage your inner critic.

4. *Learn from your inner critic*

Have a chat with your inner critic, be curious and see what you can learn from it. Believe it or not, your inner critic is often giving you clues about what you need to do to move forward. For example, maybe you are applying for a new job and your inner critic tells you something like: *"You're wasting your time – you don't have enough experience to do this job."* You could nod along and say: *"Yes, little voice in my head, you are absolutely right. I don't have enough experience to do this job."* Or you could say: *"Wait a minute. Let's look at the evidence."* This will drive you to create an overview of all the skills, knowledge, and experience that demonstrate exactly why you are the perfect person to apply for this job.

Alternatively, you might think: "You know what, little voice in my head, you are right. I don't have enough experience to go for this job. On Monday, I'm going to talk to my manager. I will discuss how I can take on more people management responsibility. I'm going to make sure I get the experience that I need for when this type of opportunity comes up again."

You might find that your inner critic is comparing you to other people. It is saying: "Look at Suzanne in the sales team. She is always so prepared when we meet with the CEO. I must look so unprofessional compared to her." Instead of spiralling into thoughts about appearing unprofessional, listen to what your inner critic is telling you and prepare thoroughly for your next meeting with the CEO. You could analyse Suzanne's performance and understand what she does that you find so impressive. Is there anything that Suzanne does that you would like to incorporate into your own style of presentation?

If you detach from your immediate emotional response to your inner critic, you can use that information positively. This will allow you to develop and grow.

Managing Imposter Syndrome

Most people have felt that creeping dread that they'll be 'found out'; like the people you work with are going to discover you are nowhere near as good as they think you are. Merriam-Webster dictionary defines imposter syndrome as:

> *"Persistent doubt concerning one's abilities or accomplishments accompanied by the fear of being exposed as a fraud despite evidence of one's ongoing success."*

In the real world this looks like:

- **You believe others overestimate your skills**. You think you've fooled others to get here. For example, you successfully complete a project. Your manager is praising and congratulating you. They might even be discussing your next role. Meanwhile, you are thinking that the project's success was just luck. There's no way you could do it again!
- **Having an intense fear of being found out.** This is particularly common when you start a new job or have been promoted. You ask yourself at what point they will discover that you don't have the skills or experience to do the job. You are just waiting for somebody to appear and say it's all been a big mistake.
- **Attributing success to factors outside of your own talents.** You may say things like, "We were lucky things went so smoothly," or "it's all down to the team," or "it was really X who did all the hard work," rather than owning your part in the success.

If any of this sounds familiar, it's important to know that you are not alone. According to a survey by Clare Josa, author of *Ditching Imposter Syndrome,* 62% of people struggle with imposter syndrome daily or regularly.[14] This is enough for it to have a measurable impact on their performance and their health. That 62% is two-thirds of the working population! The next time you are in the office or on a Teams call, look around and appreciate that two-thirds of the people there will struggle with imposter syndrome at some point that week.

Imposter syndrome is effectively a set of beliefs you hold about your skills and abilities not being good enough somehow. It takes work to unpick these beliefs as they are deep-rooted and formed as we grow up. As an adult, you can look at these beliefs objectively and take some immediate practical steps to help manage and control your imposter syndrome.

Understand that imposter syndrome is a fleeting feeling rather than a permanent state. I used to get very cross with the label 'imposter syndrome'. Not always, but sometimes it felt like people were using it as a reason for not taking chances with their careers. "I didn't go for the promotion because my imposter syndrome got the better of me." At times, it felt like a bit of a cop out. I can appreciate that imposter syndrome is a term people know and understand. It can be a useful label to express how somebody is feeling. However, the word 'syndrome' implies a chronic illness. It suggests that you need to live with it forever. This is not the case. Those feelings of being an imposter are just that – feelings.

Our thoughts create our feelings. If we go back one step further, our beliefs influence our thoughts. It is completely possible to challenge and change the beliefs that we hold about ourselves. In which case it is entirely possible to change our thoughts and our feelings. Just because we feel like we are an imposter at a point in time does not mean it needs to be a permanent feeling. We can take control and shift what we believe, what we think, and how we feel.

To help you take control of those imposter feelings, it's important to admit to yourself that you are experiencing them. In the past, we might have been encouraged to push on through and to fake it until we make it. I don't think that is a particularly helpful strategy. Instead, I would encourage you to notice and recognise exactly how those feelings of being an imposter present themselves. Do you feel nervous in the pit of your stomach? Do you feel reluctant to speak up? Do you allow others to take control of conversations? Do you speak louder to cover up the fact you are experiencing those feelings of being an imposter?

When you start to recognise your behaviour pattern when imposter syndrome kicks in, you then know your cue to do something different. For example, when you start to feel that fluttery feeling in the pit of your stomach, you know that you need to take a couple of moments to breathe deeply. Remind yourself of all of your past successes. If you are reluctant to speak up, remind yourself that your opinion is valid. Others want you to be part of the conversation.

Talk to others about what you are experiencing. We must normalise the feelings of being an imposter. Remember the stats. If two-thirds of people experience that feeling of being an imposter on a regular basis then you are most definitely not alone. As the saying goes, a problem shared is a problem halved. Talking about how you feel can help you gain a sense of perspective.

Remind yourself of your capabilities. You can't experience imposter syndrome without having achieved some success, because if you're in a position where you feel you're 'punching above your weight', it shows you must have gotten somewhere in the first place. People don't feel like imposters in perfectly ordinary situations that they can handle. People experience imposter syndrome when they're stretching out of their comfort zone, which in itself means you have gone out and done something.

The evidence log you created in Chapter 4 can be helpful. When you have difficult moments and self-doubt kicks in, you can go back and reflect on the evidence that you can make a valuable contribution, you can achieve great things and you can be successful. When you create a log of your achievements, you're not just doing it to blow your own trumpet. You are creating a record of fact that you can go back and review. This will help you feel more confident when you need it.

Get comfortable with discomfort. This is not easy; however, you are human, so at some point you will make mistakes. If you acknowledge that you are a flawed human, then there is nothing for people to 'find out'. You know that you are not perfect and that's okay.

Celebrate the discomfort. If you don't feel discomfort from time to time, chances are you are playing it too safe with your career. When you feel comfortable, it means you are doing things that are familiar to you. When you feel discomfort, you are stretching out of your comfort zone and challenging yourself. This is how you will learn and grow.

Changing your Career Beliefs takes time. However, if you are aware of your beliefs and their impact, you can control and change them. As you change the limiting beliefs that hold you back and form more supportive beliefs, your Career Confidence will grow.

In a Nutshell

- Career Beliefs are what we think is true about our ability to create the career that we want.
- Generally, beliefs are formed in childhood and develop throughout adolescence into early adulthood. They are influenced by experiences, the people around us, our culture and upbringing, and the society we live in.
- Supportive beliefs will boost our Career Confidence, whereas limiting beliefs will hold us back. Beliefs are not set in stone and can be changed.
- You can question your beliefs by asking:
    - Is that true?
    - Is it absolutely true?
    - What happens when you believe that thought?
    - Who would you be without that thought?
    - What will you believe instead?
- Once you have decided on new more positive beliefs, you can gather evidence to reinforce those beliefs.
- Your inner critic is the unhelpful voice in your head that articulates the limiting beliefs you hold about yourself. You can take control of your inner critic by: getting to know the stories it repeatedly tells you; giving it an identity to dampen your emotions when those thoughts kick in; asking it what it needs from you; and learning from it.
- Imposter syndrome is when you doubt your abilities and fear that

you are going to be exposed as a fraud. Imposter syndrome is a feeling rather than a permanent state. You can manage these feelings, remembering you are not alone, sharing your experience, and reminding yourself of your capabilities.

Chapter 7

Your Career Behaviours

"Behaviour is the mirror in which everyone shows their image."
Johann Wolfgang von Goethe

Our behaviour is how we conduct ourselves on a day-to-day basis. It's what we do and the way we act. A large part of the impression we make on other people is because of our behaviour. Relating to our career, behaviour is how we conduct ourselves at work and our attitude towards our career. As we talked about in Chapter 2, the modern workplace is evolving all the time. Our success will not be determined solely by our skills and qualifications. The way we show up and approach our career matters. Our Career Behaviours go far beyond technical expertise and encompass a wide range of actions and attitudes. They influence the opportunities that are made available to us and play a pivotal role in predicting our career success.

Anna is a Programme Manager responsible for delivering a large-scale IT implementation. Anna has two Project Managers on her team, Martin and Dave. Martin and Dave both have a first-class degree from a prestigious university, both have an Association for Project Management qualification and also both have 10 years of industry experience. However, Anna has a completely different experience working with Martin than she does with Dave.

Martin excels at project planning. He can take a complex project with many dependencies and distil it into an easy-to-understand project schedule. His timelines are ambitious, but he knows that if everyone does what is required of them, they will hit their deadlines. Martin creates his project plan, and then informs his stakeholders of what he needs them to do and by when. When milestones are missed, he complains to Anna that people are not doing what they have been told to do. He blames other people that the project is not going according to plan and is unlikely to be successful.

Dave is also exceptional at project planning. His starting point is to get his stakeholders together to understand what else is going on in their world. This way they can plan out the project collaboratively. Dave's project timelines are usually longer than Martin's. He checks in with each of the stakeholder teams on a weekly basis so that he has early sight of any project slippage. If he thinks there's going to be a problem, he consults with Anna. They agree on what work needs to be prioritised and what can be pushed back.

If you were Anna, who would you rather work with? It's pretty obvious working with Dave would be easier. While it might seem like it will take longer to complete his project, his collaborative and flexible approach is more likely to bring about long-term success. The outcomes that we deliver at work are important. However, the way we deliver those outcomes is arguably just as crucial.

In your day-to-day interactions at work, you will come across people who you hold in high regard. Reflect now on somebody you admire at work. This could be somebody you currently work with or somebody you worked with in the past. List the behaviours that the person you admire exhibits.

Think about somebody you do/did not enjoy working with. List the behaviours the person exhibits that caused you to not enjoy working with them. What can you learn from these observations? Are there particular behaviours that you are drawn to or that put you off?

What Energy Do You Bring?

Oprah Winfrey is credited with coming up with the Drains and Radiators Theory. Her proposition is that people can be divided into two categories: the drains and the radiators.

Drains are negative people who suck the energy out of others. They have a pessimistic outlook on life. After you've spent time with a drain, you feel depleted and diminished. You might start the conversation bright and positive. However, the drain's negative energy and attitude make you feel dull and frustrated. If you spend time with pessimistic people who are constantly worrying, you are more likely to do the same. Negative energy is contagious!

It's not necessarily the drain's fault. They are not deliberately trying to make you feel this way. It is just the energy they give off. However, their general outlook on life is such that they pass on that negative energy to those around them. Their years of experiences and beliefs have created layers of negativity embedded in their personality. They often feel powerless and can see their career as something *happening to them*, rather than something *within their control.*

Radiators on the other hand are people who smile and the whole world smiles with them. They have an infectious enthusiasm. They are inquisitive and playful and have a way of making others feel good about themselves. They have a genuine curiosity about other people and about what is possible in their career and life. The energy they radiate is like rays from the sun.

If you spend time with upbeat and supportive people, you're more likely to become upbeat and supportive yourself. This enables you to feel positive and confident about navigating your career journey.

You deserve to be surrounded by radiators and you don't need to let the drains in your life sap all your energy. Who drains your energy and who lights you up?

We can't change the drains in our life, but we can decide to minimise the time we spend with them. If we do need to spend time with drains, we can choose to remain light-hearted and not let their negativity affect us. We can also choose to spend as much time as we possibly can with the radiators in our life so we can spark off their positive energy.

How can you be a radiator and pass on positive energy? Can you create a ripple effect of positivity to build an uplifting, supportive working environment?

Understanding Your Career Behaviours

Ultimately, people work with people. Sheryl Sandberg summed this up by saying:

> *"Motivation comes from working on things we care about. It also comes from working with people we care about. In order to care about someone, you have to know them... I don't believe we have a professional self from Mondays through Fridays and a real self the rest of the time. That kind of division probably never worked, but in today's world, it makes even less sense... It is all professional and it is all personal, all at the very same time."*

In short, Sheryl Sandberg is encouraging us to be ourselves. The way you behave, and the way you show up is how people get to know the real you. As Johann Wolfgang von Goethe said: *"Behaviour is the mirror in which everyone shows their image."* So, how do you show up? Let's do some analysis of your Career Behaviours by identifying those now.

Take some time to reflect on how you show up in the workplace. Which of these positive and negative behaviours do you exhibit regularly?

Positive behaviours

Reliable	Creative	Delegates effectively
Adaptable	Flexible	Resolves conflict
Outcome oriented	Resilient	Respects diversity
Organised	Diplomatic	Enthusiastic

Accountable

Strong work ethic

Positive attitude

Actively listens

Shows empathy

Takes ownership of mistakes

Problem solver

Decision maker

Gracious in success and failure

Emotionally intelligent

Good at building relationships

Critical thinker

Team player

Demonstrates loyalty

Shows gratitude

Respects diversity

Recognises and celebrates achievement

Takes on leadership roles

Fosters a collaborative work environment

Fosters a positive work culture

Willing to share knowledge

Emotionally resilient

Mentors others

Balanced work and personal life

Handles criticism constructively

Negative behaviours

Procrastinates

Poor time management

Disorganised

Lacks initiative

Poor communication skills

Ineffective listening

Excessively complains

Doesn’t take initiative

Ignores constructive criticism

Lacks enthusiasm

Refuses to collaborate

Takes credit for others’ work

Lacks empathy

Avoids confrontation

Overly confrontational

Competes rather than collaborates

Doesn’t delegate

Disregards work/life balance of others

Lacks attention to detail

Unable to prioritise

Overcommits and underdelivers

Indecisive

Overreliance on others

Lacks self-awareness

Overly competitive

Lacks cultural awareness

Unable to manage conflict

Interrupts others	Defensive	Discriminates
Resistant to change	Micromanages	Lacks strategic thinking
Lacks accountability	Bullying	Poor problem-solving skills
Unreliable	Doesn't take responsibility for mistakes	Lacks creativity
Unable to see the big picture		

Now you've identified your behaviours at work, think about the areas you would like to improve.

- What can you learn from reviewing your positive and negative behaviours?
- Are you the type of person you would want to work with?
- What positive behaviours are you most proud of?
- What negative behaviours are you willing to commit to change?

You might be wondering if it's even possible to change your negative behaviours. Perhaps you exhibited those behaviours when you were growing up and all the way through your working life. Is it possible to change now? I want to remind you about the concept of neuroplasticity that we talked about in Chapter 6 in relation to changing your beliefs. Your brain has the incredible capacity to rewire itself. As you practice positive behaviours, your brain will develop new neural pathways so that over time they become your autopilot response in situations. It won't happen overnight, but you literally can 'train your brain' to change the way you behave.

Three Key Behaviours for Career Success

I have highlighted 60 positive behaviours that will help you achieve career success. But I want to delve deeper into three overarching themes, which I believe will set you up well for career success:

- Be proactive
- Be kind
- Be adaptable

1. Be proactive

When new graduates ask me how to make a great first impression in the workplace, I always tell them to 'be proactive'. This is true for people at all levels in an organisation. Proactive people recognise they are responsible for their success. They focus on what they can control. They take the initiative to influence people and their environment and choose how to respond and behave.

When you are proactive about building your career, you won't only respond to opportunities, but actively look for and go after them. In Chapters 3 and 4, we focused on getting clear on what you want from your career. If you haven't yet identified what you want from your career, go back, and do that now. You cannot proactively build your career if you don't know what you want to build!

Once you know what you want, tell other people! This might sound incredibly obvious, but many people don't do it. Be strategic about who you tell. Who needs to know what you want? It might be a line manager, a mentor, a performance manager or maybe all the above.

There's no point moaning with your friends in your lunch break when they are not in a position of power to help you get it. Nobody cares about your career or career development more than you. With that in mind, you need to take responsibility and be brave enough to ask for the things you want.

When asking for what you want, be polite and assertive rather than making demands. Nobody owes you anything. Think about how the other person or the business as a whole will benefit from you getting what you want. State your case clearly and demonstrate the benefit to your organisation.

For many people, asking for what they want carries a lot of shame. When you were a child, maybe you asked for what you wanted and were promptly reprimanded by a grown-up. Maybe in your family or even your culture, you were told that you had to make do with your lot in life. The way we feel about asking for what we want is complicated. It is heavily influenced by our personal beliefs, upbringing, and past experiences. So, if you find it difficult to ask for what you want, reflect on why that might be the case. Work to unravel why you feel the way you do and what you want to feel instead.

Similarly, many people don't ask for what they want because they want to keep a façade of being in control and doing everything perfectly. For example, you might want some help to build your network. However, you might not want others to think you aren't already well-connected.

Others might hold back from asking for what they want because they are scared things will go wrong. For example, they don't put their hand up for a project because they are scared of messing up, even though it could be a great growth opportunity.

Keep noticing when you are brave enough to ask for what you want. Keep noticing when you hold back from asking for what you want. Ask yourself why you are doing that. Keep acknowledging your successes. Celebrate when you are being brave. Over time your confidence will grow until asking for what you want will become second nature.

As well as pursuing what you want from your career, you can also be proactive in your current job role. Pay attention to what is going on around you. Keep your eyes and ears open for opportunities to get involved in interesting projects, add value, grow, and develop.

Stay updated on industry trends. Become somebody that people know, like, and trust. When you see a problem, take initiative, and develop potential solutions. Identify how to apply new thinking and ways of working in your role. When you are given a task to do, follow through and get it done. When you spot an opportunity or a project that interests you, ask to get involved. When things get challenging, stick with it. When you think it's time for a change, reflect, learn, adjust, and do things differently.

Your immediate line manager will influence how proactive you can be in your current role. If your line manager doesn't give you this kind of autonomy or empowerment (and unbelievably this happens more often than you might think!), then look for mentors or other leaders who do. When you are looking for your next role, keep in mind how much your new line manager will encourage and support a proactive approach.

2. Be kind

In today's society, there's a lot of talk about being kind, but not a lot of people walking that talk. Be kind and show empathy to the people you work with. You have no idea what people are dealing with. Understand that everybody comes to work with their own set of challenges and experiences. Acknowledge other people's feelings and be supportive of the challenges they face. Also, be kind to yourself. We are often our own harshest critics. We wouldn't treat our friends and colleagues the way we treat ourselves.

Being kind to others...

Share credit and acknowledge the contribution of others: A team's success is a collective effort. Be generous in giving credit where it's due. Publicly acknowledge the contribution of your colleagues. Not only is this the right thing to do, but it will also boost team morale. By leading by example, you can encourage a culture of appreciation and collaboration across the entire team.

Be a team player: Treat the people you work alongside with respect and empathy. People are more likely to collaborate when they feel free to express their ideas and opinions without fear of judgement and you'll be seen as a supportive team member who people want to work with. This will help you to build your reputation within and outside the organisation.

Building a supportive environment: When people feel valued and appreciated, they are more likely to be engaged in their work. Acts of kindness, whether big or small, contribute to a positive work environment. A kind word or a supportive gesture can go a long way to boosting spirits. A positive atmosphere encourages people to give their best and make a positive contribution.

Being kind to yourself...

When you treat yourself with kindness and compassion, you send a signal to other people about how you expect and desire to be treated. In Chapter 6, we talked about taking control of your inner critic. Another way to show kindness to yourself is to set healthy boundaries so that work doesn't take over your life.

Boundaries are physical, mental, digital, emotional, and environmental constructs. They create a framework that influences how we behave, what we take responsibility for, what we let in, what we keep out, and our relationships with ourselves and everything around us. Put simply, boundaries are a way of protecting ourselves. They also show how much you value yourself and the message you send about how you want to be valued.

Without boundaries, you might feel at the mercy of others and have little control over your own time. I know that a lot of my clients experience a huge amount of resistance to setting boundaries. Even just saying the word "boundaries" may sound harsh and unwelcoming. It conjures up images of a fence or a wall, a hard division that cuts you off from other people. For many of us, it can feel instinctively uncomfortable to put these divisions in place. We can worry about what other people will think. We may feel selfish when we set clear boundaries, a feeling that may worsen when we enforce them.

There are different types of boundaries that you can put in place: boundaries around your time, limitations on expending energy, and guidelines around how to protect yourself from the emotions of others.

Time boundaries

These boundaries are meant to protect your limited valuable time in your working day. This is the most tangible place to begin setting boundaries for yourself at work.

Stick to your hours: Pre-pandemic, this meant leaving the office at 5:00 pm. In a work-from-home environment with a flexible schedule, it can be tempting to try to squeeze more hours of work into your week. Some people think this will make them more productive. Even if your hours vary, it is vital to set your own expectations of what you are asking of yourself each day. If your calendar says that you are working from 9:00 am to 5:00 pm, then work those hours — and only those hours.

Create a routine that works for you: One positive outcome of the pandemic is that employers are now more comfortable with flexible working patterns. Working from home is now widely accepted. However, many employees are working longer hours because there is no delineation between home and work. Work is also increasingly creeping into their leisure time. Agree your work routine with your line manager and your team. Let them know when you are available, when you will be offline, and how best to communicate with you.

Stop checking your email when you're "off": I can't count the number of times I've gotten an out-of-office reply to an email. Then, a few minutes later, I receive a response from the colleague who is supposedly on holiday or not working. I know the temptation is to just 'take a quick look', but all those quick looks add up. If you need to check your email when not working, set a specific time to do so. This is far less intrusive than checking your phone constantly throughout the day.

The next category of boundaries to consider are the things you can do to protect your energy.

Energetic boundaries

These boundaries focus less on the hours you work, more on the effort and energy you expend during those working hours.

Stop when it's good enough: Not everything you do has to be perfect. I'm going to repeat that for the perfectionists amongst you. Not everything you do has to be perfect. You need to be able to accept when you have done enough. You've proofread the email five times, triple-checked the spreadsheet, or whatever task occupies your focus. I challenge you to stop when you have reached 'good enough'. Resist perfectionist tendencies. This can feel uncomfortable to begin with and you can feel exposed. I promise the quality of your work is probably better than you think it is. And anyway, people are very forgiving of small mistakes.

Get all the facts before you say yes to something new: The desire to people-please and jump right in has gotten the better of me more than once. When you receive a request to be involved in a new project, get as much information as you possibly can before saying yes. Are you the only one who can get involved, or are there other team members who can help? Could one of the junior team members learn from this, or must you do the work? If you've been assigned something without the option to decline it, get all the information as soon as you can. This will help you set realistic expectations for yourself and others.

Be realistic — out loud: If something doesn't seem feasible to you, say so. Build the habit of voicing your perspective at work. Let people know what is realistic for you to achieve. If you are asked to take on a project that you know is going to leave you feeling stressed and overburdened, ask your manager what you need to prioritise and identify what you will stop doing to free up your time.

Emotional boundaries

These boundaries help you manage work stress, difficult relationships, and demanding environments. They focus internally, helping with the emotional burden.

Protect yourself from others' emotions: There may be members of your team who are very stressed and anxious. It's important to make sure that, if you are not feeling stressed and anxious, you are not taking on the emotions of the people that you work with. When we spend time with people, in an intense way and at close quarters, if we are not careful, their emotions can rub off.

Protecting yourself from others' emotions might look like: reminding yourself that your experience is your own; deciding to work from a different location when emotions are running high; having purposeful do-not-disturb time where you tune out other people for a while; building in breaks throughout your working day so that you can get some fresh air and a change of scenery.

Decide your level of sociability and make your peace with that: There can be a lot of pressure to attend team drinks, lunches, and networking events. Social events can be helpful to build closer bonds and deeper relationships. However, if spending time outside of work with your colleagues is not your cup of tea, you are allowed to politely decline. You don't have to be the life and soul of the party. You might find it helpful to consider how these events fit into your life. When you have quieter periods of time outside of work, you might consider attending more of these events. Then when you have a busy period in life, you know that these types of events will need to take a back seat.

Know that you are more than your work: Take a moment to let that sink in. You are more than your work. One of my clients recently had a lightbulb moment; in fact, it was as if Blackpool Illuminations had just been switched on. We were talking about her values and the things that were important to her, when suddenly the penny dropped. Up until that point, she had been assuming that her work had to fulfil all her values. Her current work situation was far from doing that. Indeed, the lack of fulfilment made her frustrated and angry. Her breakthrough moment was when she realised that she could fulfil the needs she had and satisfy her values outside of work. She was putting high expectations on her career, and it didn't need to be that way.

Setting boundaries – whether related to time, energy, or emotions – will conserve your energy and allow you to make a more meaningful contribution at work. Rather than seeing them as a career behaviour that restricts the contribution you make, you can see them as a powerful tool that allows you to enhance your performance.

3. Be adaptable

We know that the only constant is change. We also know that the pace of change in the coming years will be faster than ever before. Being adaptable will be crucial in this ever-evolving professional landscape.

Technology is reshaping industries at an unprecedented pace. Automation, artificial intelligence, and other disruptive technologies are fundamentally altering the nature of work. The people who can adapt to these changes will stay relevant and competitive in the job market. They can do so by acquiring new competencies.

Industries are also transforming. Economic shifts, geopolitical events, and global crises impact sectors in unforeseen ways. The Covid-19 pandemic promoted a surge in digitalisation across many industries. The people who adapted quickly to this new way of working demonstrated the importance of being flexible and open to change. They turned challenges into opportunities for growth.

As you progress in your career, you may also discover new passions, interests or strengths. These may lead you to move in unexpected directions. Being adaptable will allow you to pivot and explore new avenues. It prevents stagnation and ensures continued engagement and enthusiasm for work. Instead of waiting for change to happen, we all have a responsibility to anticipate and prepare for it. This forward-thinking approach will position you as a leader and 'one to watch'.

In a Nutshell

- Our Career Behaviours are how we conduct ourselves at work and also in wider career settings.
- The energy that you bring is important. You can either be a drain leaving others feel depleted and diminished or a radiator who brings an infectious enthusiasm.
- Understanding our own behaviour is crucial. You will have positive behaviour traits that you will be proud of and similarly negative behaviour traits that you will want to change.
- Three key behaviours for career success are: being proactive in your current role and seeking opportunities for development; being kind to yourself and others; being adaptable to account for the constantly changing nature of the world we live in.

Chapter 8

Your Career Brand

"Brand yourself for the career you want, not the job you have."
Dan Schawbel

What do other people say about you when you are not in the room? Your Career Brand, also known as a personal brand, is about identifying how you want to be known by other people and how you portray yourself, both consciously and unconsciously. You could hope that the good work you do and the reputation you have built because of that good work speaks for itself. However, in a busy, crowded world, you need to have a proactive strategy to influence what people know, believe, and say about you. Building a positive Career Brand will make it easier to obtain support from others to help you achieve your Career Vision and Career Goals.

Think about how corporate branding works. We associate specific feelings, values, and expectations with brands we trust. Every company has a story and an image. As soon as you see the Apple logo, you immediately think of innovation, sophistication, and a passion for technology. The Nike swoosh conjures up images of inspiration, focus, and above all winning. The Virgin brand has expanded across a plethora of industries; regardless, it is associated with disruption, adventure, and success in the face of adversity.

Career branding is no different. While you don't necessarily have a logo, when people hear your name, what immediately comes to mind? Whether you are aware of it or not, you are sharing your Career Brand with the world every single moment of every single day. Every interaction you have with your colleagues, your boss, and your clients reflects your Career Brand. The question is whether you are doing yourself justice and whether these interactions are representing you in the most positive light.

Working on your Career Brand doesn't mean changing your entire personality or representing yourself as something you are not. The single most important thing you can do when building your Career Brand is to be yourself. It does mean getting clear about the impression you want to make and ensuring your attitudes, behaviour, and communication reflect that.

The Power of a Career Brand

Many of my clients are hesitant to engage in career branding. They think I am asking them to start posting their lunch on social media and become TikTok influencers. They don't see the value of spending time building their Career Brand. Surely, they just need to focus on doing their job? Unfortunately, it's no longer enough to do good work to get on in your career. You need to do good work *and* let other people know about the good work that you are doing. If you are not telling people about your achievements, then you could be missing out on opportunities for career advancement.

There is nobody who cares as much about your career as you do. Therefore, you need to be the one putting in the effort to spread the word. and explain why you should be top of mind for career opportunities. If you think of one standout memorable person in your current organisation who you admire, I'm sure you can identify why they are top of mind for you. What observations can you make about their Career Brand?

In today's hyper-connected and competitive world, career branding is more than a buzzword. It's a strategic necessity. With your own career in mind now, career branding allows you to:

Differentiate yourself in a crowded market

Your organisation and others like it are jam-packed with talented professionals. To advance your career, you need to stand out and differentiate yourself from the competition. Career branding allows you to highlight your unique skills, experiences, and perspectives. You are unique. Ultimately, that is what is going to make you stand out.

In the earlier sections of this book, you clarified your skills, strengths, and experiences. As you construct your Career Brand story, you will showcase all your unique qualities. This will help you stand out among the many talented individuals in your peer group. A distinct Career Brand will make you memorable to colleagues, superiors, and clients. This will increase your chances of being chosen for important projects and promotions. It will also allow you to build your reputation, expand your networks, and access opportunities in your wider industry and beyond. Finally, building your Career Brand will give you a competitive advantage, as you can guarantee that at least 80% of your peers aren't doing it.

Advance your career progression

Career branding isn't just about getting noticed in your current role. It's a powerful tool for career progression. A strong Career Brand can open doors to new opportunities. It may lead to promotions and leadership roles. It could also result in speaking engagements or panel discussions at industry events. Employers often seek out employees who can represent their company effectively. If you want to be front of mind, people need to know who you are.

Build trust and credibility

A well-crafted Career Brand allows you to showcase your expertise, integrity, and reliability. Colleagues and superiors are more likely to trust and collaborate with you. Clients and collaborators are more likely to engage with you if they see you as an expert in your field. By positioning yourself as a thought leader in your field, you can influence and shape conversations within your industry. By showing up in a consistent way, you will build a reputation that others can rely on.

Networking and relationship building

Effective networking is a key part of long-term career success. When you have a well-defined Career Brand, you know who you are and the value you bring. You also know the story you want to tell about your career success. This makes networking so much easier. Your Career Brand can be a conversation starter, allowing you to establish meaningful connections inside and outside your organisation. You are better able to connect with like-minded professionals, mentors, and potential collaborators. People are naturally drawn to those who have a clear sense of purpose and expertise.

Futureproof your career

In Chapter 2, I shared research by the Institute of the Future. They say that 85% of the jobs that will exist in 2030 didn't exist in 2019. It's almost impossible to predict how your career might progress and what you will end up doing. However, a strong Career Brand can help you stay relevant and resilient as industries evolve. By continually learning, growing, and showcasing your ability to adapt, you become a valuable asset to your organisation. This applies to any organisation you wish to join, especially during times of change or uncertainty.

How to Build Your Career Brand

You have already done some of the key groundwork required to build your Career Brand, such as understanding your strengths, values, interests, and Career Goals. If you haven't done those things yet, then I'd strongly suggest you go back and do them. Otherwise, you could be doing a lot of misdirected work that could find you building the wrong Career Brand!

1. Identify what you want to be known for

The first step in building a Career Brand is to define what you want that brand to be. Reflect on your strengths, values, and long-term goals for your career. What do you want to be known for in your industry? You may want to be known for your deep subject knowledge; as a functional expert; having exceptional project management skills; being able to build relationships at all levels; or connecting people who would benefit from knowing each other. Consider the things you do naturally without thinking about them. These make up your unique selling point and the qualities that set you apart from your peers.

2. Create your Career Brand Manifesto

Your Career Brand Manifesto sets out what is important to you that people need to know about you. You can use the following questions to help guide your thinking:

- What unique skills and capabilities do you have to offer the world?
- What is your current reputation among colleagues and your network?
- What three words sum up how you want to be perceived?
- What do you want other people to say when they interact with you?
- How do you want people to feel after they have spent time with you?

For example, my Career Brand Manifesto is as follows:

> *Hi, I'm Nicola, I help my clients to build their confidence, achieve their Career Goals and find fulfilment and happiness at work. I'm well-positioned to help my clients because once upon a time, I was exactly like them. The first half of my career was spent as a Business Change Consultant at large professional services firms. I enjoyed working for these organisations and was incredibly good at my job, but there was always something not quite right. I wouldn't say I was a square peg in a round hole. More like a bumpy round peg in a smooth round hole! I now work with professionals who feel like a*

bumpy round peg in their professional life to build a career based on their version of success. When I work with people, I focus on the three Cs:

Clarity: to identify what they want

Courage: to be brave enough to go after it

Compassion: to be kind to themselves along the way

People describe me as being infectiously driven and straightforward. I've also been called an iron fist in a velvet glove, which I took as a compliment! My interpretation is that I am supportive and empathetic while holding my clients to account to make sure they achieve their goals.

Now it's your turn. Write your own Career Brand Manifesto to share what you want the world to know about you.

3. Create your Career Brand Statement

Your Career Brand Statement distils your Career Brand Manifesto into a concise and compelling statement. It conveys the value you bring and your goals for your career. Your aim is to make this statement as memorable as possible. My Career Brand Statement is very simple:

I'm Nicola Semple, a Career and Confidence Coach, I help people to wake up in the morning looking forward to the day ahead and go to work with a spring in their step.

Other examples are:

I'm Emily Johnson, a human resource specialist. I'm known for fostering inclusive workplaces and cultivating leadership talent. I have spent the last few years leading the way. I created inclusive policies for IVF, fertility treatment, menopause, and domestic abuse. I'm always open to sharing my experience if it's relevant to your organisation.

I'm John Casey, a public relations specialist. Some call me The Secret Door Opener because I use my little black book to get my clients in front of people who can make a big impact on their business. I work with retail businesses in Scotland to secure press and media coverage. This helps more people discover their amazing products.

I'm Zoe Green, an independent financial adviser. I mainly help women who have recently gone through a divorce to get their financial affairs in order. I help them understand their options. I also support them to make decisions that will allow them to be financially secure and have peace of mind.

Your Career Brand Statement should sound natural. It is important to phrase it using words you would normally use. There is a big difference between words being written down on a page and the spoken word. Be sure to practice saying it out loud. You might even find it helpful to record it as a voice note or a video.

Once you have crafted your Career Brand Statement, get feedback from mentors and colleagues. Do they understand the message you are trying to convey? If not, then simplify and refine your statement. Once you are happy with it, print it off and pin it up in a prominent place, or save it as a note on your phone. The key is to return to the statement regularly and practice it. This way, you get comfortable with the words and can easily share them with other people.

First impressions matter. When you meet somebody for the first time, it's important that you can competently and confidently articulate what you do and the value you bring. Your Career Brand Statement gives you a way to do this that you can repeat and reuse.

Write your Career Brand Statement now and ask for feedback from three to five people.

4. Identify who you want to be known to

Creating a Career Brand is not about shouting about who you are and what you do with the entire world. Be strategic and consider who you want to know about you and what you have to offer. This could be inside your organisation. It could also be within your industry. Perhaps, it's in your wider community.

Who needs to know about you? Who do you want to know about what you have to offer? Think about organisations you would like to work for. Also, consider professional bodies, industry specialists, sponsors, and senior managers within your own organisation.

Compile a list of people you want to know about you. Think about the most effective ways to build relationships and get yourself in front of these people.

5. Share your story

Once you are clear on what you want to be known for and who you want to be known to, it's important to start sharing your story. The foundation of an excellent Career Brand is doing good work. However, doing good work on its own is not enough. You need to get into the habit of sharing the good work you are doing.

Sharing your accomplishments may not come naturally at first, but think of it like building your self-promotion muscle. When you first start going to the gym to train, it feels awkward and difficult. Over time, you build the habit. You get used to working the different muscles in your body. Over time, you learn to push yourself further and further.

The same is true of building your self-promotion muscles. The more you practice, the easier it becomes. And the more you practice, the more comfortable you get pushing through the discomfort. You also put yourself in more situations where you can share your achievements and the great work you are doing.

Overcoming Resistance to Building Your Career Brand

You've read all the compelling reasons to build your Career Brand and maybe you still think: *"Nope, not doing it. It's yucky and icky. When I see other people doing it, it makes my skin crawl!"* If this is you, let me help you get some perspective.

At its most basic, career branding is sharing who you are, what you stand for, and what you have achieved with the world. This seems very straightforward on the surface. However, for some people, it is incredibly difficult. You might find it challenging to share what you believe in and what you stand for because you fear judgement from other people. You might be concerned that people will laugh at you or not take you seriously. You might compare yourself to others in your organisation or your industry, believing your ideas are not as worthy or that you are not as experienced or advanced as them. You might have grown up in a culture where it was not the done thing to talk about your own achievements. Maybe you grew up in a family where your parents bragged about every single achievement, so you decided that you were never going to follow in their path.

Despite all this, self-promotion matters, especially in a career context. If you do not self-promote, you risk falling behind peers who are shouting from the rooftops about their achievements. You need to make sure that the right people know about your accomplishments. If you haven't flexed your self-promotion muscles before, it can take a bit of training to get going. But once you start and do some regular self-promotion activities, you will find it gets easier over time.

Google set up the #IamRemarkable[15] initiative to encourage self-promotion among women. They have now expanded the initiative to encompass not just women, but all under-represented groups. I'd highly recommend that you look it up. I was so impressed with the work they do that I trained to be an #IamRemarkable facilitator. Now I run workshops on their behalf, pro bono.

At the start of the training, one sentence became an absolute gamechanger for me. It was this: "It's not bragging if it's based on fact."

I hated the idea of self-promotion because I didn't want to appear like I was bragging. Understanding that it's not bragging if it's based on fact shifted how I felt. Have you worked on a successful project, earned a promotion, or received an award? If so, why not share it with others? We are sharing successes that are based on fact. Successes that are real and solid and meaningful. What is the point of an award if it's not shared. The whole idea of awarding people is to show recognition, which intrinsically assumes a person is doing the recognising. We are not only celebrating our achievement, but also inspiring others about what is possible for them.

Understand Your Career Brand 'Why'

To help overcome your resistance to building your Career Brand, spend some time thinking about why you are doing it in the first place. What is your overall Career Vision and how does building your Career Brand fit within that? For example, if your objective is to get promoted in the next 12 months, you have a clear goal to work towards. It can motivate you. You can then think about the narrative that you need to create to support you to get this promotion.

- What skills and attributes do you particularly want to highlight?
- What stories can you share that reinforce your knowledge and experience?
- Who do you need to get your message in front of so that you can have maximum impact?

Getting clear on your why makes it much easier to get off the starting blocks. You can then get out in the world and share your message.

If you are based in the UK, you may have heard an advert on the radio for the Macmillan Cancer Charity. The voiceover shares the story of a day in the life of a Macmillan employee. They talk about the range of ways they support their clients, for example, setting up a bed outside so that a dying patient can see their dog or arranging a taxi for a cancer patient after a gruelling chemotherapy session. They share the incredibly invaluable work they do and explain they wouldn't be able to do this work without donations from the public.

Every time I hear the advert, I think it is a fabulous example of how you can use your 'why' to drive action. Rather than feeling uncomfortable asking for donations, they know it is necessary to fund their work. The Macmillan employee knows the incredible impact that can be made because of donations; therefore, they have no problem asking for them.

That's how I want you to think about self-promotion. Be clear about what you want to achieve. Know that you're taking action to reach your goal. At first, you might not enjoy sharing your achievements, but the more you do it, the easier it will become.

Why is sharing your Career Brand important to you? What do you want to achieve as a result of sharing your Career Brand?

Using LinkedIn to Build Your Career Brand

There are a lot of LinkedIn lurkers who spend time on the platform and consume other people's content, yet are reluctant to raise their heads above the parapet, build connections and share their own content online. However, when used properly, it can be an exceptionally powerful tool to help you build your Career Brand.

As of September 2023, LinkedIn had 983 million members in over 200 countries. That's about one-eighth of the world's population. Additionally, about 134.5 million users actively used LinkedIn each day.[16] Don't worry, you don't need to connect with all 983 million members! But I hope you can see the potential to access and leverage this vast professional network.

1. What do you want to achieve by using LinkedIn?

If you approach LinkedIn as something you feel you *should* be doing rather than having a clear intention and purpose for spending time there, your efforts will be half-hearted. You may find you spend a lot of time there for very little reward. Like most social media platforms, LinkedIn can be a huge time suck. It's important to be intentional about your purpose for using the platform.

- Do you want to find a new role?
- Do you want to position yourself as an influencer within your industry?
- Do you want to build a network of people in a similar profession?
- Do you want to build a network of people who live in your area?

Keep in mind that your intentions may change over time. Your short-term intention may be to use the platform to research new roles. Over time when you have secured a new role, you may widen your intention to building a network in your specific industry.

Set some short-term intentions now for using the LinkedIn platform.

Over the next three months, what is your top priority for building your Career Brand on LinkedIn? Once you have identified your immediate intention you can then set up your profile accordingly.

2. Review your LinkedIn profile

If you don't already have a LinkedIn profile, it's time to set one up. If you do already have a profile, take the opportunity to update and optimise it. Your LinkedIn profile needs to paint a picture of you and your achievements. It also needs to position you in a way that will best allow you to achieve your goal. If we reflect on the quote from Dan Schawbel at the start of the chapter, "Brand yourself for the career you want, not the job you have". Craft your LinkedIn profile to summarise your experience and also reflect on where you want your career to go.

Keywords

Identify keywords that people you want to connect with may use to search on LinkedIn. Use them throughout your profile. For example, if your intention is to build up a network of professionals in Bristol, you would need to use the word Bristol multiple times in your profile. If you want to network within a specific industry, you should ensure that industry appears often in your profile.

Headline

Your LinkedIn headline is the short summary that appears underneath your name. It should cover who you are, what you do, and how you get results. You can use this space to share your job title, for example, Talent Leader. However, that doesn't tell the reader much about the work you do. Instead, "Helping develop the leaders of the future through coaching and training" gives a better idea of what you do. To maximise impact, play around with your LinkedIn headline until it reflects the work you do and the value you bring.

Summary

Another important piece of your LinkedIn real estate is your summary section. This is your chance to showcase your key skills and achievements. Consider what you want to be known for and reflect this in your summary. Keep in mind any keywords that will be important for people to use to find you in the search function. I always encourage clients to avoid formal language in this section. It should sound as though they are speaking to the reader. Imagine you met somebody at a networking event. You wouldn't introduce yourself in a formal, stilted way. Instead, you would talk to them like a human being and express your personality and creativity.

Top tip: When writing your summary section, spend time considering your opening three sentences. Make them compelling enough for people to click to read more.

Bonus top tip: Make it easy for people to contact you. Include an email address or telephone number in your About section. This allows people to connect directly.

Experience

The Experience section on LinkedIn is an online CV where you can detail the roles you have held. In this section, don't just list your responsibilities, outline your achievements. When possible, also make these achievements quantifiable.

Recommendations

Ask people you have worked with in the past to write you a recommendation. This is an excellent way to build credibility and gather social proof of the impact that you make.

Graphics

Make your profile more compelling and attractive by including appropriate graphics:

Profile picture: Your profile picture should be recent enough to reflect your current physical appearance. It doesn't need to be a formal headshot although it does need to be appropriate in a professional capacity. No photos of you with a margarita in hand on the beach on holiday!

Header image: You can create a header image using free software such as Canva. The image should reflect you, your skills, and your personality. To get information on the latest size guidelines and best practices for LinkedIn headers, type "Create a LinkedIn header" into your search engine.

Vanity URL

You will probably find that your LinkedIn URL is a string of letters and numbers. This makes it tricky to share your link with other people.

LinkedIn allows you to customise your profile URL to make it easier to share. These so-called vanity URLs can be customised to include your first and last name. This can also make your profile easier to find online. You can edit and create your custom URL using your account settings.

Type "Customise your public profile URL" into your search engine. You will find the most up-to-date instructions to change it.

3. Build your LinkedIn connections

Now that you have your up-to-date LinkedIn profile in place, you can start to build and grow your network. Again, it's important to be intentional about this. There's no point in sending out connection requests to hundreds of people without thinking about why you want to connect with them.

Join groups relevant to your industry or profession. Contribute frequently. Notice who else is interacting in these spaces. Would they be good people for you to connect with? Strike up conversations in the comments and then send an invitation to connect.

Follow relevant organisations. Identify companies that you would be interested in working for or that you admire and follow their company page. This can be a great way of building up your industry knowledge and means you will be able to keep an eye on any jobs that are advertised.

Connect with former colleagues and peers. As you move from one organisation to another, LinkedIn can be a useful way to keep in contact with old colleagues. Also, as your old colleagues expand their network, you will have the opportunity to connect with even more people in your industry.

Comment on posts your connections publish on LinkedIn. This allows you to strike up conversations with your connections and also raises the profile of their content with people in your network. You can also start or reignite relationships by sending direct messages. Perhaps you come across a piece of industry research that you think would be useful to somebody, so you send it on. Or you may want to carry on a conversation that started in the comments section of a post.

Share content. The fastest way to get noticed on LinkedIn is to be brave and share your own content. According to a report by Kinsta, only 1% of users post content to the platform.[17] This means you're already beginning to stand out above 99% of other users on the platform just by posting. Remember to be intentional about what you share to build your Career Brand. Your content should reflect your Career Brand Manifesto and what you want the world to know about you.

Be consistent. Consistency is key. You will be less successful if you post prolifically for three months and then disappear for the next three months. If you share useful information with your network, they will notice when you aren't around anymore.

In a Nutshell

- Your Career Brand is how you want to be known by other people. In other words, what people say about you when you're not in the room.
- Career branding allows you to: differentiate yourself in a crowded marketplace; build trust and credibility; progress in your career; network and build relationships; position yourself as a thought leader; demonstrate your adaptability and resilience.
- To build your Career Brand you need to: identify what you want to be known for and to whom, then share your story.
- Self-promotion and sharing your Career Brand can feel uncomfortable to begin with, but becomes easier the more you do it.
- LinkedIn is a powerful tool for building your Career Brand. You can build a compelling profile that will demonstrate the value you bring and create a targeted network of connections to support you to achieve your Career Vision.

Chapter 9

Your Career Village

"Alone, we can do so little; together, we can do so much."

Helen Keller

There is an African proverb, popularised by Hilary Clinton in the 1990s, that says: *"It takes a village to raise a child"*. The phrase conveys the message that it takes many people (the village) to provide a safe, secure environment for children to develop, flourish, and realise their hopes and dreams.

In a similar fashion, I believe it takes a village to build a successful career. We need a Career Village, a community of people to interact with and support us. This community will help us fashion a career that satisfies us and allows us to fulfil our potential. In return, we each have a responsibility to be supportive members of other people's Career Village. This will help us support others to create a career that provides them with fulfilment and satisfaction.

Your Career Village is made up of several components:

- Your immediate team
- Your wider organisation
- Your own board of directors
- Your role models
- Your career buddies
- Your personal support network

Your Immediate Team and Wider Organisation

The people you work with on a day-to-day basis are the most obvious and immediate aspect of your Career Village. In the first instance, this is your team. These are the people who you spend time with daily. To a certain extent, your individual success may well be tied to the overall team's success. In a broader context, there will be a wider community of people in your organisation who you won't work with directly, but who also contribute to the success of the whole.

A few things to consider in relation to the people on your team and in your organisation:

- What are you doing to nurture productive and healthy relationships with your team members?

- How would you want your manager to describe you to their peers?
- Who in your organisation can support your career journey?
- How can you support others within your team to achieve their Career Goals?

Your Own Board of Directors

You may have come across the idea of creating your own personal board of directors. Your board of directors is a group of people that you can consult with and gain support from when navigating your career.

Your board of directors will inevitably change over time as your career evolves. You won't tell most of them that they're on your board. It would be rather embarrassing if you decided to demote or remove somebody!

Members of your board could be:

The Industry Expert: These people have deep professional, technical, or industry experience and can give you access to knowledge that you don't have. They may also connect you with other experts who can support you.

The Idea Generator: These are the people who push the boundaries of your thinking and always come up with innovative and often surprising ideas. They are excellent at cross-pollinating ideas across industries and areas of expertise. The Idea Generators bring energy and buzz. They encourage you to make unexpected connections.

The Master of Getting Stuff Done: These are the people who have the uncanny ability of making the seemingly impossible possible. They have a good grasp of your organisation's politics and know how to cut through barriers and red tape. They can help you do the things you want to do quickly and effectively.

The Connector: They are somebody who makes introductions and connects you with useful people. Connectors are people who know everybody; and if they don't, then they know somebody who does. They can help you expand your network and help you get to know people you would not otherwise have access to.

The Critical Advisor: This is somebody who will challenge your decisions and help you see your blind spots and where you are going wrong. They help break you out of your habitual ways of thinking. When choosing a Critical Advisor, don't shy away from challenging people. Keep in mind that receiving their challenge may feel uncomfortable at first but will give you a better result in the long run.

The Positive Pusher: This person always has your back. They strengthen your resolve during tough times and remind you of your original reasons for doing something. They help you stick with decisions even when the going gets tough. When choosing a Positive Pusher, you can include people from any part of your life – at work or outside. However, they absolutely must believe in you and what you can achieve.

The Sanity Checker: The Sanity Checker keeps you grounded. They hold you to account to help you achieve balance between work and the rest of your life. They care about your wellbeing, and they want you to stay true to yourself and what you hold to be important. These are the people you can call when you are losing perspective and need a reminder of the importance of balance.

The Sponsor: The Sponsor is one of the roles on your board of directors that requires consent from the other person. A Sponsor speaks out to advocate for you and your ideas to senior or important people. They make it a point to publicly endorse you and champion your work. They need to be on board with this and happy to speak up and support you.

It is important that you navigate your relationship with your Sponsor effectively. They are voluntarily giving their time and energy to support you and your career. Most importantly, by backing you, they are putting their own reputation on the line. If you mess up, it reflects badly on them.

Creating Your Own Board of Directors

Have a think about who you currently have on your board of directors. You may not have thought about them this way before. However, people in your network likely fulfil some of these roles.

- Who are the experts you rely on, either for industry or functional expertise? Do you have somebody in your network who always inspires you? Do they give you a fresh perspective when you spend time with them? Do they help you see problems in new ways?
- Who do you know that always comes up with great ideas? Who is

that person who has a leftfield brainwave that solves the problem you have been grappling with?

- Who is your influential Master of Getting Stuff Done? Who can effortlessly navigate politics and instinctively knows how to make things happen?
- Who do you know that is an incredible Connector who allows you to tap into their network to help you build your own?
- Do you have someone who gives you honest feedback, no matter how uncomfortable or difficult it might feel?
- Can you identify a Positive Pusher? Can you always rely on someone to spur you on and give you that extra motivational nudge to achieve your goals?
- Who is your Sanity Checker who keeps you grounded and helps you to maintain balance in your life?
- Do you have a Sponsor? How often are you in contact with them and are they clear about what you want from your career right now?

As you build your Board of Directors you will be able to access different types of support as and when you need it.

Your Role Models

Role models are people who you admire and who inspire you. You might not have direct contact with your role models, and they might not even know you exist. However, they play an important role in your career. These people could have already walked the path you want to walk. They could be senior leaders in your organisation or in your wider industry, or they might be business leaders in your local community. Your role models could even be the authors of books you have read or people you have listened to on a podcast, watched being interviewed, or the owner of social media accounts that you follow.

To give you an example, one of my role models is somebody I follow on LinkedIn. I have regularly interacted with his posts, so he probably has a vague awareness of who I am. However, as we work in very different industries, it's unlikely our paths will ever cross in any meaningful way. I enjoy the content he shares, and I find him interesting. I love the way he naturally and genuinely shares about his life and his family. It makes me feel like I know him. In terms of an example of career branding done well, he is my role model! I look at his content and I think about how I can put that into practice in what I share on my own social media accounts.

- Who do you consider to be a role model?
- How do you stay in touch with that person, so you can continue to draw upon their influence and be inspired?

Your Career Buddies

Your career buddies are people at a similar career stage who 'get' the stage of career and life you're in. They are in a similar place themselves. They could be friends from university or perhaps they started out in the same organisation as you in your first job. You have probably added to and grown your group of career buddies over the years. You now have a merry band of current and ex-colleagues, whom you consider friends.

Together, you share inspiration and advice about your personal career journeys. These are the people who will help you celebrate your promotions and commiserate when things don't go your way. They will have your back and support you every step of the way if you decide to change careers.

When life gets busy, it can be easy to let those relationships slide. It can feel indulgent to catch up with your career buddies when there is much else going on in your life. You don't need to meet up with them on a weekly or even a monthly basis. But if you can't remember the last time you caught up perhaps it's time to get something scheduled into the diary or at least reignite the conversation in your WhatsApp group.

Your Personal Support Network

Your support network is often overlooked, but it's a vital part of your Career Village. These are people who give you practical support in all aspects of your life, which in turn can help you be successful in a work context.

Your support network can include your partner, family, friends, and childcare providers. It may also include a cleaner, housekeeper, or gardener. This is your behind-the-scenes team. They take some of the pressure off you and free up your time and headspace to devote to your career. These are the people who can reduce your mental load and take care of the 'stuff of life'.

On a practical level, if you have children and a partner, you will need to agree who is responsible for specific childcare tasks, like meal planning, cooking, and supervising homework. If your children are young, you will have some formal childcare, such as a childminder, nursery, or wraparound care at school. If you have older children, you may rely on them to support with caring for younger siblings.

If you don't have an adequate support network, it will inevitably have a detrimental impact on your career. You will have to spend time, energy, and attention ensuring that these aspects of your life are kept under control.

A few questions to consider:

- Who is currently part of your support network?
- Do they understand the importance of the role they play?
- Do you show them appreciation for their support?
- Where are the gaps in your support network where you are devoting more of your own time than you would like?
- How can you fill the gaps in your support network?
- What practical actions do you need to take to make that happen?

Mapping Out Your Career Village

Putting it all together, let's map out who is currently in your Career Village. Identify any gaps and think about how you could potentially fill those gaps.

If you don't know how to do that at the moment, that's okay. You have planted the seed of the idea in your brain. In the coming weeks and months, with the help of your reticular activating system(!), you will start to encounter people who can fill the gaps in your Career Village.

Building Your Career Village Through Networking

When it comes to networking, people fall into one of two camps. Those in the first camp love networking. They see it as an opportunity to meet new people, have interesting conversations and make potentially useful connections. Those in the second camp would rather dig their eyeball out with a blunt pencil and have it served to them as a pre-dinner canape than go to a networking event.

Regardless of the camp you fall into, networking is important. It can be a phenomenal way to accelerate your career success, but only if you do it properly. At its simplest level, networking is just people getting to know each other and identifying ways in which they can help each other. This isn't about having awkward conversations at big events. It's not about going on the hunt to gather as many business cards as possible. This is about making connections and building enduring, mutually beneficial relationships. Since you have worked on your Career Brand in Chapter 9, you will be clear on how you help people and how you want to be helped.

How to network

The goal of networking should be to help other people. Yes, it would be nice if they helped you out as well, but networking is a two–way street.

And your side of the street is all about helping others, not asking them to help you. Only ask for their support after learning about the person and providing value.

It's far more important to understand their needs before you tell them about yours. Your goals should not be at the front of your mind. You're trying to develop a relationship with someone, which means you should be thinking about them. It's your job to understand the people in your network, where they are coming from and what's important to them. Be open-minded and curious. Ask questions and listen to what people have to say.

Where to network

There are lots of different ways that you can build your network:

Networking events and conferences: These are probably the types of events that spring to mind when you think of networking. They may be specific to your industry or your area of functional expertise.

Online networking platforms: The best-known professional networking platform is LinkedIn. However, there are also other industry-specific forums out there. You can join these platforms to participate in relevant groups and discussions. You can also share insights and connect with professionals in your industry.

Professional associations (either specific to your industry or profession): These organisations often host networking events, seminars, and workshops. You get a chance to meet like-minded individuals from outside your organisation.

Mentorship programmes: Your organisation may offer a mentorship programme. You can also find external programmes. They connect you with experienced professionals who can offer guidance and support. These relationships can provide access to valuable opportunities.

Ongoing professional development: Participating in relevant ongoing professional development allows you to enhance your knowledge and skills. You can also meet people with a common interest.

Alumni networks: These clubs can be educational or professional. They are a great place to meet people who share a sense of camaraderie, making it easier to establish connections.

One-to-one meetings: You can set up informal one-to-one meetings with existing contacts to build on the relationship, or you can set them up with people you find interesting and want to learn more about.

It's important that you find a way to network that feels right for you. If you feel uncomfortable or anxious in large crowds, then don't go to a conference with 500 people. Find something smaller. Hone your networking skills there before going to a large event.

Networking face-to-face

When you decide to attend a networking event, be clear on your objective for attending. Perhaps you want to build your network to support you in your current role. Maybe you want to discover future roles. Maybe you are attending because you are interested in the topic or the speaker and you are keen to attend for your own personal development. Your purpose for attending the event will help you clarify who you want to meet and the types of interactions you want to have.

Get your logistics sorted. This includes start times, travel information, venue details, what you're wearing, and the weather forecast(!), so that everything can run as smoothly as possible on the day.

Find out who is attending. If you can, get hold of the attendee list before the event. You can start to connect on social media with anybody you are interested in meeting. This can be a great way to break the ice so that when you meet them face-to-face you will already have had an online exchange.

Maximise the opportunity to meet new people. If you are going to the networking event with a colleague, set some ground rules. It's great to have that feeling of safety in numbers. However, you don't want to spend the entire time speaking to somebody you already know. If you are going to the event on your own, don't spend the entire night hiding in the toilet. Look around the room and spot somebody else who is on their own. If there are no other lone attendees, look out for groups of three. It's much easier to join in with a group of three than with two people who are already engrossed in conversation.

Make a good first impression. When you meet somebody for the first time, they will form an opinion of you within seconds. Use the Career Brand Statement you created in Chapter 8 to introduce yourself succinctly and in a way that encapsulates who you are and what you do.

Introduce people. Develop the habit of introducing people. Connecting like-minded people is a powerful way to enhance your network. The idea of doing this seems foreign to many people, but it is actually quite easy. Do you know two people who went to the same university? Or like the same sports teams? Or work in the same industry? You get the point. Don't make it hard. Just introduce the two of them by sharing their common interest. They can decide if they want to pursue the relationship further.

Connect people. Ask if people want to be connected to other people in your network. If you think there is somebody in your network who could help your new acquaintance, ask if they would like to be connected. Even if they aren't interested, they will appreciate the offer.

Follow up. After the event, make sure you find a way to stay connected to the people you've met and would like to meet again. Follow up within 48 hours – before people forget who you are. This could be a LinkedIn connection request, an email or, if you want to be very brave, a phone call. Make sure that whatever you have committed to do in conversation, you actually do. For instance, if you say, "I have a great article on that; let me send it to you," then do send it. You can then nurture this relationship over time. Comment on their LinkedIn posts, exchange occasional direct messages, send useful resources, and recommend future events that you are attending where you could potentially meet in person again.

Once you get comfortable and find the types of networking events that you enjoy (or can best tolerate!), you will find it is an incredibly valuable way to cultivate and grow your Career Village.

In a Nutshell

- Your Career Village is the group of people who support you to build your career.
- Your Career Village is made up of: your team (your peers, reports, and your manager) who you interact with daily and people in your wider organisation; your own board of directors who you can consult with (even from a distance) when navigating your career; role models who inspire you; peers who provide moral support and celebrate success; and your support network, people who help make the other aspects of your life happen so you are free to focus on your career.
- Networking is an excellent tool to build your Career Village. You can network via events, online platforms, professional associations, educational experiences or by setting up meetings. It can feel uncomfortable at first, but the most important thing is to be yourself and offer value before asking other people for anything.

Chapter 10

Your Career Balance

"Balance means making choices and enjoying those choices."

Betsy Jacobson

In today's fast-paced world, work-life balance is a hot topic as we strive to achieve equilibrium between our professional and personal lives. When I started to write this chapter, it took me a while to settle on the word "balance". The dictionary definition of balance is "equal distribution of weight, amount, etc". Surely, there are many factors outside our control. It is unrealistic to expect an equal distribution of our time and energy between work and home life.

At first, I liked and considered the idea of work-life harmony. The dictionary defines "harmony" as a "consistent, orderly, or pleasing arrangement of parts". There is something about the word that implies peacefulness and tranquillity. Yet since it also suggests that you always have your act together, this is another unrealistic expectation to manage.

Other ways of expressing this constant challenge of successfully navigating work and life are: work-life blend, work-life fit, and work-life integration. All good words but each with their drawbacks. Both "blend" and "integration" imply fluidity and lack of boundaries between work and home, which I don't think is good for anyone's mental health. Work-life integration was getting closer, but it sounded clinical and technical.

In the end, I decided to stick with Career Balance, because while the term is not 100% correct, it is widely recognised. We all understand what we mean when we talk about work-life balance.

Whatever you want to call it, the basic principle remains the same. Work should be an element – albeit an important one – of your life, not the sole focus of it. The way that your work and personal life interact will change over time. As we talked about in Chapter 4, we go through seasons.

The quote from Betty Jackson at the start of this chapter sums this up. She said: *"Balance means making choices and enjoying those choices."* Balance is not better time management, but better boundary management. We constantly have to choose what we focus on. There will be seasons where you are able to and will want to devote more time, energy, and attention to your career. In other seasons, life outside work will take priority.

The Difficulty With Finding Career Balance

Getting Career Balance doesn't mean switching off our laptop at 5:00 pm every day. It also doesn't mean sticking to 35 hours a week, every single week. It means making decisions about what is important to us at a certain point in time, focusing on those things, and reviewing and recalibrating as required. Sounds easy, doesn't it? However, we all know that finding Career Balance is not straightforward. There are good reasons for it.

Ambition

Ambition can be all-consuming. The drive to achieve a specific goal may lead to long hours, extensive travel, and a high level of commitment. It can also mean prioritising work above everything else. When we are operating in this state, especially with colleagues and co-workers in a similar position, it can be difficult to remember the bigger picture of life and where work fits in.

The 24/7 Work Culture

The 24/7 work culture is fuelled by global business and time zone differences. This means that work never ends, which makes it difficult for individuals to disconnect and relax. They feel the need to stay connected to work at all hours of the day and night.

Evolving Mobile Technology

Evolving mobile technology allows us to work anywhere at any time. It has facilitated the 24/7 work culture. Smartphones and email keep us constantly connected. This makes work creep into our personal lives. The constant notifications, social media, and digital distractions can make it hard to focus on our personal lives. Work is tantalizingly calling to us through the screen. The temptation to check that email when your phone pings while making dinner can lead to an hour's worth of work that could have waited until the next day.

Economic Uncertainty

The post-Covid landscape and subsequent economic uncertainty play a significant role in shaping the work-life balance narrative. In a competitive job market, individuals might feel compelled to go above and beyond out of fear they will be the ones to go if cuts are required. This leads to longer working hours, increased work-related stress, and less downtime outside of work. This makes them put their professional obligations ahead of their mental and physical wellbeing.

Cultural and Organisational Norms

Workplace and cultural norms significantly influence the pursuit of Career Balance. In some cultures and industries, long working hours are expected and rewarded. This makes it difficult for individuals to opt for a more balanced approach to work and life. The 'hustle culture' is often glorified. People are encouraged to work hard, even at the expense of their physical and mental health. As a result, the idea of taking time to prioritise your personal life may be met with disapproval.

Why is Finding Career Balance So Important?

Finding the elusive Career Balance may be tricky but it is important. We know that Career Balance leads to:

Decreased burnout and increased ability to manage stress

The United Kingdom is no stranger to stress-related issues in the workplace. According to the Health and Safety Executive, over 875,000 workers in the UK experienced work-related stress, depression, or anxiety in 2022/2023.[18] This is the reported number. I would counter that the actual number is significantly higher. Many employees conceal mental health symptoms due to lingering stigma about revealing these issues.

Stress has significant personal repercussions. It also poses a financial burden on the economy. A report published by Mental Health Foundation and London School of Economics and Political Sciences found that mental health problems cost the UK economy at least £117.9 billion annually.[19]

According to a study by Mind,[20] a UK mental health charity, a poor work-life balance is one of the leading causes of stress. In their survey, 60% of respondents reported that working long hours affected their mental health. They are also at greater risk of stress and burnout. In contrast, those who successfully manage their work and personal lives are less likely to suffer from these issues. They also have higher levels of emotional resilience.

Increased productivity

The UK's Advisory, Conciliation and Arbitration Service[21] emphasises that having time for relaxation and pursuing personal interests can boost creativity and problem-solving abilities. Finding a proper work-life balance allows individuals to recharge and return to work with a fresh perspective and new ideas. This ultimately improves productivity.

Improved job satisfaction and performance

If you have found a manageable balance between work and life, it makes logical sense that you will be happier in your work. It's also more likely to encourage you to stay with your current organisation.

Research from the Chartered Institute of Personnel and Development[22] shows that a lack of work-life balance is a leading factor in employee turnover.

A survey by Gallup[23] in the UK found that engaged employees are 17% more productive than their disengaged counterparts. When people feel supported in their personal lives, they are more likely to invest their best efforts in their professional roles.

People are happier

When life isn't solely focused on work, people have the space and freedom to set and pursue personal goals and hobbies. Achieving these goals boosts self-esteem and provides evidence of personal growth and development.

A healthy work-life balance allows you to invest time in nurturing personal relationships. Strong social connections provide emotional support and a sense of belonging. They also offer an avenue for personal growth through shared experiences, learning from others, and developing empathy and communication skills.

Defining What Career Balance Looks Like For You

Balance is highly individual, so it's important to identify what it looks like for you in your career. To help you do that, I want to introduce you to the Capacity vs Capability Conundrum.

Your capacity is what you are able to get done over the course of a day, a week, a month. It's effectively what you can fit into your life. Your capability is your qualities and abilities. Think about your capacity in terms of a bucket. For some people, that bucket will be a huge vat, perhaps the size of a barrel where whisky is stored to mature. For other people, that bucket will be a little pail that a child would use to make a sandcastle at the beach. You need to understand the size of your own capacity bucket.

Your capacity is influenced by things like your caring responsibilities and your mental and physical health. You will find that the size of your capacity bucket will change over time. It's important to be honest and understand what your capacity bucket looks like at any given moment and understand why your capacity bucket is that size.

Maybe your capacity bucket is a huge shiny red trug bucket. It's so big you could plant a tree in it. It is robust and has handles on either side, so you can pick it up and move it around. You've spent time focusing on your physical health. You are brimming with energy. Mentally, you are in a good space. At the moment, the only person you need to look after is yourself. You know you have the capacity, time, space, and energy to take on new projects both at work and outside it.

On the other hand, perhaps your capacity bucket is more like the size of a washing-up basin you can fit in a sink. Your immune system has been running low and you've caught every winter bug that has been circulating leaving you feeling permanently exhausted. You're spending a lot of time caring for your elderly mother, who has just had a hip replacement, leaving you less time for everything else you need to do.

In both examples, the capacity buckets are significantly different sizes and there are good reasons for the difference in size. Your capacity bucket is what it is at this point in time. There are things that you can do to support yourself and make your bucket bigger. For example, get more sleep, take a vitamin supplement, or get support with your caring responsibilities. However, cramming more and more into your bucket, thinking that you will just have to cope, is not going to be helpful.

This can be very challenging for some people. They start to compare themselves and wonder why others can take on more than them. Feeling the pressure to please others, they take on more and more until their capacity bucket is overflowing. They just don't want to let other people down.

The next thing to think about is your capability. There are lots of things that you can do, but just because you *can* do them doesn't mean you *must*. The trick here is recognising your own capacity, acknowledging, and celebrating your capability, then deciding what is important to you. What's so important to you that it will be allowed space in your capacity bucket? Make sure you put those things in your capacity bucket first.

This is where you will devote your time, energy, and attention. If we did all the things that we're capable of, we could fill our time 24 hours a day, 7 days a week, and then some! That's why you need to focus on the things that are important to you right now. Make sure you use your capacity to make them happen.

Decide to selectively use your capability in a way that allows you to work within your current capacity. Then you start to build confidence that you are able to make the right choices for you.

To create a visual representation of your Career Balance, you can draw your own capacity bucket. Make a note of the things that currently influence the size of your capacity bucket. Reflect on what is currently filling your capacity bucket. What makes your capacity bucket overflow and causes you to feel overloaded and stressed?

Reprioritising to Achieve Career Balance

If you find your capacity bucket is consistently overflowing, you will need to reprioritise so you can achieve the Career Balance you desire. Once you know everything you must do, the size of your capacity bucket and where your capabilities lie, you can identify what to stop and what to increase. A university professor at Harvard used this exercise to illustrate to his students the power of prioritising.

The professor stood in front of the group of high-powered over-achievers. He pulled out a one-gallon, wide-mouthed mason jar and set it on a table in front of him. Then he produced about a dozen fist-sized rocks and carefully placed them, one at a time, into the jar. When the jar was filled to the top and no more rocks would fit inside, he asked, “Is this jar full?” Everyone in the class said, “Yes.”

“Really?” he said, reaching under the table and pulling out some smaller rocks. The professor dumped some smaller rocks in and shook the jar, causing the smaller rocks to work themselves down into the spaces between the big rocks.

Then he smiled and asked the group once more, “Is the jar full?” By this time the class was onto him. “Probably not,” one of them answered. “Good!” he replied. And he reached under the table and brought out a bucket of gravel. He started dumping the gravel in and the tiny pebbles went into all the gaps left between the larger rocks and the smaller rocks. Once more he asked the question, "Is this jar full?" "No!" the class shouted. Once again, he said, "Good!"

Then he grabbed a pitcher of water and began to pour it in until the jar was filled to the brim. He looked up at the class and asked, "What is the point of this illustration?" An eager student raised his hand and said, "The point is, no matter how full your schedule is, if you try really hard, you can always fit some more things into it!"

"No," the speaker replied, "That's not the point. The truth is this. If you don't put the big rocks in first, you'll never get them in at all."

To achieve the Career Balance you desire, put the important tasks in your capacity bucket first. This ensures they get the time, energy, and attention they need. You can then put in the smaller rocks and decide whether the gravel is something you want to keep or eliminate altogether.

First, you'll need to identify the importance of the tasks on your plate.

- In the context of your career, what are your key priorities, your big rocks?
- What are the smaller rocks that also need to be in your capacity bucket?
- What is the gravel that you need to remove from your capacity bucket?

Practical Strategies to Help You Achieve Career Balance

Now that you are clear on your priorities, you can use these practical strategies to help you bring your vision of Career Balance to life:

Embrace flexibility

Employers are now much more open to flexibility in your work arrangements. Get clear on what type of flexibility would support you to achieve better Career Balance. Speak to your employer. Ask if flexible hours, remote work options, or compressed work weeks are possible for you. Be objective about your current situation and identify what would make the biggest difference. Sometimes people think working from home is the answer to all of their problems. However, they may discover that working a four-day week would make the biggest difference.

Ruthlessly prioritise

While it's important to contribute to your team, overcommitting can lead to burnout. Be realistic when assessing your workload. Your to-do list will never be complete. The simple act of clearing your inbox will generate even more emails in return. When one project comes to an end, another one will magically appear. You won't be able to tick off everything and have the satisfaction that you are 'done'. Instead, you will constantly have to juggle competing demands, which requires ruthless prioritisation.

Earlier we talked about how you need to balance your capacity with your capability. You can use the Capacity vs Capability Matrix to help you assess whether you are the best person for the job.

High Capacity/High Capability – This is a task you should complete.

High Capacity/Low Capability – You have the time to complete the task, but there will be people who could do a better job. Is there somebody more appropriate who could take on the task? If not, are you willing to accept that the task won't be completed to the highest possible standard?

High Capability/Low Capacity – Is the task urgent? If not, can it be scheduled for a point in the future when you have less on your plate? Do you need to deprioritise something else to have the time to complete this task, or are you willing to delegate the task and accept it might not be done to the standard you would like?

Low Capability/Low Capacity – This is a flat no. You don't have the time and it's not your skill set.

Decide which category each task falls into and then maintain those boundaries, as we covered in great depth in Chapter 7.

Look after yourself

You cannot separate your physical and mental wellbeing from your ability to do your job. If you want to be your best at work, you need to be your best in life as well. This means taking time to look after yourself. You can do this by eating a balanced diet, getting regular exercise, and establishing healthy sleep patterns. Taking time away from work to pursue your passions and interests will leave you feeling refreshed and energised.

Career Balance in a Hybrid World

The opportunity to work from home, even for part of the working week, helps many people to better manage their work and family commitments. Achieving a balance between your career and life in a hybrid working environment requires careful consideration. It also needs an intentional approach.

Create a clear separation between work and home

With no commute and no clear physical separation between work and home, there can be a temptation to let work and life blend. So much so, that you never switch off. To help you create a clear separation between work and home, designate a specific area at home as your workspace. This recreates the physical separation between the office and home. This makes it easier to mentally switch between work and personal activities. It also sends a clear signal to others in your household that when you are in that space, you are not to be disturbed.

Adopt a consistent routine

To minimise the risk that you get out of bed, decide to 'check your email', then find yourself at 6:00 pm in front of your laptop still in your pyjamas with a selection of dirty plates cluttering your desk, it's important to give your working day a structure. Establish a routine that includes working hours, proper breaks, and dedicated personal time. You can take advantage of working from home by scheduling exercise into your day. Mark the time in your calendar like you would a meeting. This helps create a regular rhythm to your working week.

Establish rituals to transition from work/life mode

When you work in an office, you establish rituals that signify the start and end of the working day. Perhaps it's buying a morning coffee as you walk to the office. Maybe it's locking away your laptop in a drawer before you leave in the evening. When you work from home, you can create your own rituals that signal the beginning and the end of your working day. Perhaps you take a walk around the block before sitting down at your desk in the morning or end the day by writing your to-do list for the next day. Embedding these rituals into your day will help you mentally transition between work and personal life and create a sense of closure.

Use technology mindfully

Today, your mobile phone has more computer power than all of NASA back in 1969 when it placed two astronauts on the moon![24] How incredible is that? We can use technology to be more productive. It can also help us have more freedom and flexibility to work anywhere.

However, we have to set restrictions on our digital communication. Otherwise, it will take over our life, become a source of constant distraction and impact our mental health. Monitor and be mindful of your use of technology. Identify ways that it will allow you to streamline tasks and work more efficiently. Turn off non-urgent notifications to minimise distractions.

Make the most of the opportunity

For many people, hybrid working becoming normal has been their long-sought holy grail. If you can truly control your work schedule and location, you can create a work pattern and routine that accommodate caring responsibilities and other family commitments. You can structure your day to take advantage of your energy highs and lows. It also allows you to think about your time holistically and find ways to be as productive as possible.

For example, if you know that a trip to the Post Office on a Saturday morning is going to take you an hour, but on a Wednesday morning, the traffic is lighter, parking is easier and the queue is shorter, then take advantage of the opportunity to get more done in less time.

Your Career Balance Will Change Over Time

Like all aspects of your career, regularly re-evaluate what a good Career Balance looks like to you. As your circumstances evolve, your needs will change. As your professional circumstances evolve, what is possible will change too. Regularly evaluating and readjusting will allow you to keep your Career Balance in check.

In a Nutshell

- Your Career Balance is the equilibrium between your professional and personal life.
- Career Balance means making decisions about what is important to us, focusing on those things and recalibrating as required.
- While a laudable concept, finding Career Balance in reality can be tricky because of: personal ambitions, increased global connectivity, the 24/7 work culture, throwbacks to the traditional version of success, economic uncertainty fuelling the need to ensure job security, cultural and organisational norms encouraging a long-hours culture.
- Career balance is vital as it ensures:
  - Less burnout and greater ability to manage stress
  - Increased productivity
  - Improved job satisfaction and performance
  - Happier people
- Career Balance means different things to different people. You need to identify what balance looks like for you. This requires you to balance your capacity with your capability.
- To achieve Career Balance you need to: embrace flexibility in your work arrangements; establish career boundaries with your colleagues and clients; learn to say no to other people; look after your physical and mental wellbeing; prioritise ruthlessly.
- Career balance in a hybrid world requires careful consideration

including: creating a clear separation between work and home; adopting a consistent routine; establishing transitions; mindful tech use; making the most of the opportunity!

- Your definition of Career Balance will change over time and you will need to flex and adapt accordingly.

Chapter 11

Your Career Confidence Plan

Now that you have worked through all aspects of the Career Confidence Wheel, you can decide where you are going to focus your attention and create a plan to build your Career Confidence.

Your Career Values – Getting clarity on and prioritising your Career Values will help you to identify what is important to you about your work. You will identify the non-negotiables that you need to be happy and fulfilled at work. You will also create criteria against which you can assess all future career decisions.

Your Career Vision – Creating your Career Vision will help you articulate what career success looks like to you. You will have clarity on what that looks, sounds, and feels like. Having this compelling vision will motivate you to work towards your version of career success. What will that look, sound, and feel like?

Your Career Goals – Selecting your Career Goals will give you specific milestones to work towards over the next 12-18 months. They will help to get you focused and taking action so that you can bring your Career Vision to life.

Your Career Beliefs – Knowing your supportive and limiting Career Beliefs will help you to identify what might trip you up and stop you from doing the work to become career confident. Over time you can let go of the beliefs that don't serve you and instead build a set of beliefs that will support a more confident version of yourself.

Your Career Behaviours – Understanding your current Career Behaviours will allow you to identify where you may be holding yourself back and what behaviours you may decide to change. Identify the behaviours that will help you to build a satisfying and fulfilling career and practice these behaviours until they become second nature.

Your Career Brand – Developing your Career Brand will help you to identify what you want to be known for. It will also allow you to be strategic and focus on who needs to know about the great work you do and how you can easily let these people know about it.

Your Career Village – Building your Career Village will allow you to create the support network that you need to help you achieve your goals. You can also become part of other people's Career Village and pass on your support to others.

Your Career Balance – Defining your Career Balance will allow you to be productive without burning out. It will ensure you make your career a priority but not at the expense of other aspects of your life.

- Which of the elements of the Career Confidence Wheel is going to be your highest priority over the next three months?
- What actions will you commit to so that you can improve your score on the Career Confidence Wheel?
- What timeframe will you commit to completing these actions?

Monitoring and Reviewing Your Progress

I know that you are busy. One minute it's Monday morning and in the blink of an eye, it's Friday afternoon. In the intervening period, you are busy, busy, busy. If you are not careful, your commitment to build your Career Confidence could end up on the scrap heap next to your commitment to going to the gym three times a week and drinking 2 litres of water every day.

That is why you **must** schedule time each week to monitor and review the progress you are making towards building your Career Confidence. If you don't look back and identify what you have achieved, you might not even notice how far you have come. And even if you can notice how far you have come, those achievements will not be celebrated. They are just a tick in the 'done' box and you are quickly moving on to the next task.

I would strongly encourage you to block out 15 minutes, either on a Friday afternoon or a Monday morning, to take stock of the week. You can craft a set of questions that are specific to you that you consistently ask yourself each week. It could be something like:

- What have I done to build my Career Confidence in the last week?
- What am I most proud of?
- What has been my biggest learning?
- Next week, who do I need to be to show up as the most career confident version of myself?

You don't need to write the equivalent of *War and Peace* when you answer these questions. Short and succinct is all that is required. The important thing is to build the habit of reflection and to make sure it is happening on an ongoing basis.

As a result of building up this practice of reflection, you will:

- Stay on track to achieve your goals and build your Career Confidence rather than getting lost in the busyness of your daily life.
- Regularly check in with whether you are happy and fulfilled at work and then make changes before you become completely miserable.
- Build up an evidence bank of your achievements which you can refer to when your confidence dips and you need a boost.

I wish you the best of luck on your journey to building your Career Confidence. It won't all be smooth sailing and there will be bumps along the way, but it will be worth it. Taking control of your career now means that you won't look back in 20 years' time and think "if only I had..."

Next Steps

Would you like more support to help you take control of your career and find fulfilment at work?

1. Download the Career Confidence Workbook

The Career Confidence Workbook is the free companion to The Career Confidence Toolkit. It is a fillable PDF that contains all the exercises included in this book. You can access here:
https://nicolasemple.com/workbook

2. Listen to The Career Confidence Podcast

In The Career Confidence Podcast, we explore how you can build your career with confidence and improve your workplace happiness. We cover topics such as managing uncertainty, dealing with stress, overcoming self-doubt, and building healthy boundaries so that you can excel at work and still have a life. You can access via all the major podcasting apps or listen here:
https://nicolasemple.com/podcast

3. Connect on LinkedIn

I share Career Confidence content and resources on LinkedIn. You can connect with me here:
https://www.linkedin.com/in/iamnicolasemple/

4. Work Together

Working with a coach is the fastest way to take control of your career, especially if you need help to uncover why you feel stuck or need some accountability. Find out more about my coaching services here:
https://nicolasemple.com

About the Author

Nicola has one very simple goal. For people to wake up in the morning, look forward to the day ahead, and go to work with a spring in their step.

She works with professionals who have fallen into their careers and risen through the ranks because they 'don't know what they want to do when they grow up'. She helps them to approach their work with purpose and direction and craft a career that brings them joy and fulfilment.

Nicola is a displaced Glaswegian living in Surrey with her Surinamese Dutch husband, gymnast daughter, climbing-mad son, and Etti the cat. When she's not helping clients solve their career quandaries, Nicola spends her time playing Uber driver for her two kids, cooking up a storm and planning micro-adventures with family and friends, her most recent being a day trip to Marrakesh.

References

1. Online Etymology Dictionary, https://www.etymonline.com
2. Tupper, Helen, Ellis, Sarah (2020), Squiggly Careers: Ditch the Ladder, Discover Opportunity, Design Your Career, Penguin
3. Keynes, John Maynard (1930), Economic Possibilities for our Grandchildren, Essays in Persuasion
4. Mental Health UK, Burnout Report https://mentalhealth-uk.org/burnout
5. Simmons, Michael, The Mental Model Club: https://mentalmodelclub.com
6. Institute for the Future and Dell Technologies, Realizing 2030: A Divided Vision of the Future, https://www.delltechnologies.com/content/dam/delltechnologies/assets/perspectives/2030/pdf/Realizing-2030-A-Divided-Vision-of-the-Future-Summary.pdf
7. HR Magazine, Three Quarters of Women Lack Confidence in the Workplace: https://www.hrmagazine.co.uk/content/news/three-quarters-of-women-lack-confidence-in-the-workplace/
8. Covey, Stephen, (1990), The 7 Habits of Highly Effective People, Simon & Schuster UK
9. McCormack, Mark H., (2014), What They Don't Teach You At Harvard Business School, Profile Books
10. Behavioural and Brain Sciences, Volume 24, Issue 1, February 2001, pp 87-114, https://doi.org/10.1017/S0140525X01003922
11. Colins, James, Poras Jerry (2005), Built to Last: Successful Habits of Visionary Companies, Random House Business
12. Resume Builder, One Third of Gen Zers Have Made Career Related Decisions From TikTok Advice, https://www.resumebuilder.com/one-third-of-gen-zers-have-made-career-related-decisions-from-tiktok-advice/
13. Katie, Byron, (2022) Loving What Is: Four Questions That Can Change Your Life, Rider Classics

14. Josa, Clare (2019), Ditching Imposter Syndrome: How to Finally Feel Good Enough and Lead with Courage, Confidence and Passion, Beyond Alchemy Publishing

15. I am Remarkable, https://www.rmrkblty.org/iamremarkable

16. Influencer Marketing Hub, 36 Of The Most Important LinkedIn Stats for 2023, https://influencermarketinghub.com/linkedin-stats/

17. Mindblowing LinkedIn Statistics and Facts, https://kinsta.com/blog/linkedin-statistics/#:~:text=This%20means%20that%20only%20about,most%20credible%20source%20of%20content

18. Health and Safety Executive, https://press.hse.gov.uk/2023/11/22/hse-publishes-annual-work-related-ill-health-and-injury-statistics-for-2022-23/

19. The economic case for investing in the prevention of mental health conditions in the UK, https://www.mentalhealth.org.uk/explore-mental-health/publications/economic-case-investing-prevention-mental-health-conditions-UK

20. How to Promote Mental Well Being, https://www.mind.org.uk/media-a/4662/resource3_howtopromotewellbeingfinal.pdf

21. ACAS Guide to Flexible Working, https://www.acas.org.uk/flexible-working-and-work-life-balance

22. Good Work Index, https://www.cipd.org/globalassets/media/comms/news/2023-images/good-work-iindex-executive-report-2022_tcm18-109897.pdf

23. 10 Employee Engagement Statistics You Need to Know, https://haiilo.com/blog/employee-engagement-8-statistics-you-need-to-know/

24. Your Smartphone is Millions of Times More Powerful Than the Apollo 11 Guidance Computers, https://www.zmescience.com/feature-post/technology-articles/computer-science/smartphone-power-compared-to-apollo-432/

Printed in Great Britain
by Amazon

42681846R00106